STOP IT NOW

Stop It Now

"BREAK FREE FROM SELF-DOUBT: A RADICAL APPROACH TO TRANSFORMING YOUR MINDSET, OVERCOMING LIMITING BELIEFS, AND UNLOCKING YOUR TRUE POTENTIAL"

BY SHIELA LITTLE, LMSW, PHD (C)

DEDICATION

To my sons, Khaylen, Khalil, and Nikia II,

Becoming a mother was the catalyst that shaped my life. I realized that, to raise three outstanding young men who will grow into exceptional fathers, husbands, and individuals, I needed to embark on a journey of healing and self-discovery. This journey enabled me to become a remarkable woman, equipping me with the qualities of both a nurturing and present mother. It has changed the trajectory of experiences that you have had and will continue to have. I cherish and adore each of you and am profoundly grateful for the precious gift of your presence in my life.

Thank you for inspiring me to become the best version of myself.

Loving you always,
Your Mother.

CONTENTS

PREFACE

Unmasking the False Self

A false sense of self, or an artificial persona, often emerges as a defensive mechanism from early trials, shielding us from the trauma or stress endured in our formative relationships. This 'false self' acts as a self-spun façade, typically crafted unconsciously. For years, I lived under the influence of this false sense of self. As I began the journey toward healthier, authentic relationships, I recognized its pervasive presence. This book delves into the origins of the false self and reveals the insidious impact of shame - that relentless voice whispering that we're never enough.

From my earliest memories, my false sense of self was rooted in shame and a deep sense of inadequacy. Throughout life, this manifested in the delusion that achievements, accolades, relentless work, boundless service, wealth, and possessions would make me a better, more lovable person. I believed earning more, acquiring degrees, completing endless tasks, assuming various community roles, perfecting motherhood, and owning luxury items would lead others to see me as successful, worthy of love, appreciation, and acceptance. This misguided belief held that these accomplishments could heal my soul's fractures and alleviate my inner turmoil and feelings of inadequacy. This belief couldn't have been further from the truth.

My entrepreneurial spirit emerged when I was just twelve, braiding hair, a skill my aunt taught me. I began monetizing my passion early, discovering that I could turn something I loved into income. At this tender age, I set my sights on doing more, being more. Demands piled up, especially from my family, and I eagerly rose to meet them, striving to "prove" myself. By the age of twenty-six, I juggled a successful hairstyling business, had earned a bachelor's degree, ongoing master's studies, and the responsibilities of motherhood, all while navigating a strained relationship with my then-boyfriend and my mother's mental health issues.

My career transitioned from hairstyling to a school social worker, and subsequently, I became a clinical therapist and college counselor. Alongside my expanding career and community involvement came the accumulation of material possessions, inevitably leading to crippling debt.

At the time, I didn't realize that I was accumulating not only financial debt but emotional, physical, and spiritual debts. As my spending escalated, I felt compelled to take on more therapy clients to keep pace with mounting expenses. I found myself working sixteen-hour days, volunteering for various community boards, and always at the beck and call of friends and family. The belief that more—more action, more effort, more possessions—would someday yield happiness was firmly entrenched in my psyche.

Around the age of thirty-two, it became undeniable: I was utterly exhausted on every level. My health was in shambles, and I was diagnosed with chronic daily headaches. My body revolted, rendering me unable to stand without vertigo and nausea. There were days when I couldn't muster the strength to leave my bed, yet I persevered. Deep-rooted in my core was the belief that to surmount any challenge, I merely needed to do more, say more, be more, have more, and force my way through. But life's stark evidence continued to challenge this belief—I depleted my FMLA, financial resources dwindled, relationships frayed, and I remained adrift in numbness. I felt stuck, and the time had come to wake up and initiate changes that would redirect the course of my life for good.

Today, my life bears little resemblance to its past form. I am no longer the twelve-year-old or even the thirty-something who believed that overachieving was the path to love and acceptance. I've evolved into a whole person, one who makes conscious, healthy choices, enforces healthy boundaries, and embraces the joy of living while giving myself compassion and grace when life gets strenuous, and choices are challenged. This book is an open door to my journey, a wellspring of experiences, and a roadmap for those who seek a path to healing and wholeness and who want to change their mindset and unlock their potential.

Yes, that means YOU.

You hold this book because, like me, you seek more fulfillment in life. The weight of stagnation is heavy, and you struggle to identify the root of your discomfort. You sense a higher purpose for your life, yet find yourself in limbo, possibly waiting for someone to acknowledge your value, to save you, to truly see you. So, you, like me, persist in this endless cycle of striving, doing everything for others, but feeling like you're on a hamster wheel, putting in a lot of effort yet making no progress.

As we navigate these pages together, see me as a trusted friend and an experienced guide. I am here to show you how to STOP IT NOW and take the lead in your life. You'll learn how to rewrite your life's story, moving from feeling stuck to becoming unstoppable.

INTRODUCTION

L ife is a complex fabric made from our experiences, which shape us into who we are and influence how we navigate this intricate journey. Learning to cultivate a harmonious relationship with ourselves and others is the key to a life filled with purpose, contentment, and boundless joy. This book represents my humble offering—a beacon to guide you on a transformative journey towards your best self.

In these pages, I share insights from my 18+ years as a therapist and 10+ years as a business owner, aiming to empower you with the potential for life-changing growth. The lessons here are universal, yet I hope they resonate with you personally, providing solace, inspiration, and the means to unlock your hidden potential. This book is dedicated to those weighed down by guilt and shame, who feel they haven't met societal expectations. It's for anyone seeking strength, confidence, and the realization that they are capable of being the protagonist in their life's story.

This book encourages individuals who've limited themselves, urging them to courageously chase their grandest dreams. We will learn to turn life's challenges into opportunities, embodied in the practical, memorable framework of the acronym 'STOP IT NOW.' Embark on a profound journey of self-discovery, confronting and overcoming negative emotions, beliefs, and behaviors. These are the chains that foster procrastination, self-sabotage, and impostor syndrome—obstacles that prevent achieving and maintaining your goals.

Inspired by Mahatma Gandhi's profound words, "Your beliefs become your thoughts, your thoughts become your words, your words become your actions, your actions become your habits, your habits become your values, your values become your destiny," we understand that everything starts with our beliefs. Together, we will embark on a transformative journey, moving from feeling stuck to becoming unstoppable. This journey involves reshaping our self-perception and our view of the world, enabling us to create solutions in our L.I.F.E. - Love of self, Interactions with others, Focus, and Energy.

Join me on this path of self-discovery and growth. We will rewrite our life stories, rekindle our inner spirit, and realize the destinies we've always dreamed of.

1

STOP: THE POWER OF REWRITING YOUR **STORY**

Storytelling has a profound influence. The narratives we are told and the tales we narrate to ourselves have a remarkable impact on how we perceive ourselves, make choices, and navigate our journey through life. Our minds are both impressionable and influential, often believing the stories we hear. Positive, uplifting stories can shape our lives in alignment with those narratives, while negative stories can erode our self-worth, leading to self-doubt and unfulfillment. I speak from experience. The destructive stories I encountered and internalized from childhood until my late thirties diminished my self-esteem, convincing me I was unworthy and inadequate. This belief drove me to strive relentlessly for more, in a bid to prove my worth and earn the love and acceptance I craved.

Now, I recognize the importance of understanding these narratives. Comprehending our stories is the first step in freeing ourselves from the shackles of shame and any other barriers holding us back. It's a crucial part of our healing journey.

One narrative I absorbed as a child was feeling unwanted. My mother, who had four children, often left my older brother and me at our grandparents' while keeping my younger siblings close. This led me to believe she didn't want me, planting seeds of inadequacy and driving my constant need to achieve more.

Another significant experience occurred when I was about seven. My grandmother, whom I adored, would often take me on her grocery shopping trips, even allowing me to skip school for this. We'd meticulously plan these excursions, clipping coupons and strategizing our purchases. Unbeknownst to me, my grandmother sometimes used extra coupons to reduce our bill, and my mother, who worked as a cashier in the same store, would process them. This routine, while seemingly mundane, on this day, further entrenched my feelings of being unwanted and not enough.

The day of our shopping trip always filled with excitement. Being allowed to push the cart made me feel grown-up, and I eagerly anticipated seeing my mother. Our encounters were rare, and I yearned for a connection with her. As we navigated the aisles, my anticipation mounted. When our carts were full, we headed to my mother's checkout line. My grandmother left me in the queue with some coupons and food stamps, including a few invalid ones, and went to another cashier. Approaching my mother's register, I was shocked when she abruptly closed it, referring to me as 'little girl.' This dismissal was crushing. Did she not recognize me as her daughter? The fear of having invalid coupons compounded my distress, and tears welled in my eyes, reinforcing my belief in being unwanted.

I often questioned why my mother had children if she didn't seem to want us. This incident solidified my feelings of rejection, and I resolved never to return. My two younger brothers, who spent more time with her, only deepened my sense of exclusion. It seemed she wanted them but not me, driving me to strive harder to be the 'good girl' that my grandparents would want to keep.

In my efforts to be indispensable, I assisted my grandparents in every way I could. I helped my grandmother with her medication, took on household chores, and mastered the art of cooking, a skill I treasure to this day. My grandmother had a knack for creating meals from simple ingredients like cornmeal and chicken broth. Her rice pudding, especially, became a symbol of our bond. The scent of vanilla still brings back warm memories of the love and time we shared in her kitchen.

Her kitchen was my haven. It was where she taught me to make her famous 7-Up cake. Whether I was coming in from playing curb ball, double-dutch, or spending time with my granddad in the garage, I always responded eagerly to her call. In the kitchen, I felt grown-up despite my young age. She would say, "Wash your hands and gather the ingredients." I meticulously arranged the ingredients on the counter in the order she needed them, showing I was a "good girl" who paid attention. The butter, eggs, and sugar were first, followed by the flour, flavorings, and 7-Up soda. Lastly, a few drops of food coloring. As we sang and chatted, I would ask questions, immersing us in hours of conversation and camaraderie. This was my way of showing my grandmother that I deserved her love.

Helping my granddad, a car mechanic and a jack-of-all-trades, was entirely different. He had a short temper and didn't hold back criticism if you made a mistake. At home, he reminded me of the Big Bad Wolf, capable of causing chaos with his angry outbursts. Yet, outside our home, he was beloved by his nieces, nephews, cousins, and friends.

With my grandfather, I learned about life, tools, craftsmanship, and the importance of hard work. He was always a man with a plan, though not always a successful one. He was purposeful and determined. I learned to anticipate his needs, staying three steps ahead and avoiding mistakes. If he needed a specific tool or directions for a project, I had to be ready. Having seen his temper and experienced his strict discipline, I was keen to avoid both.

During our time together, he would share stories of his life in the South, his hard work, and how much had changed since his youth. He was proud of his family's achievements: owning their land, crops, and animals. He often voiced his disdain for lazy individuals and the "white man," advocating for self-reliance. He constantly reminded me that to achieve anything in life, I had to work hard and make it happen, as no one else would. He reinforced this by sharing his experiences and highlighting that I was the only one willing to help him.

From my grandfather, I learned the value of adaptability and developed a mindset of doing and being more to avoid his disdain, which I believed he felt towards others. As a result, I did whatever was necessary, or what I thought could prove my worth. My sole aim was never to be a burden to my grandparents or any other caregiver.

However, there was a time when I began to doubt whether my grandparents really wanted me. Hearing their conversations about financial struggles and my mother's failures only added to my uncertainty. At that time, my grandparents were still supporting two of their eight children, along with my brother, my cousin, and me. Managing a household of five children on a limited budget caused significant hardships. I internalized their worries, perceiving them as directed towards me. This deepened my feelings of insignificance and insecurity, fueling my desire to become "big" or significant in some way.

My childhood was marked by experiences that deepened my self-doubt and sense of inadequacy. Interacting with my grandparents taught me the art of adaptation, of molding myself to meet others' needs. This approach became my strategy to avoid being a burden. As a child, I longed to be indispensable to those who offered me love, care, and sometimes pity.

My life's narrative was intricately woven with rejection and abandonment. The recurring disputes between my grandparents and my mother cast a shadow of uncertainty over my sense of belonging in the family. Initially, I mistook their harsh words as reflections of their feelings towards me. With time, I understood that their arguments were targeted at my mother, not me. Despite this realization, I couldn't help but internalize these conflicts, perceiving them as confirmation of my feelings of being unloved and unwanted.

As I grew older, further experiences compounded my sense of inadequacy and rejection. I faced teasing and bullying at school, mostly about my appearance. My intelligence, once a beacon of pride, turned into a focal point for mockery. These persistent taunts gradually chipped away at my self-esteem. Eventually, I started feeling ashamed of my intellect, believing it alienated me from my peers.

At the age of 10, I was faced with a major – to disclose the fact that I was being molested. I stood up for myself and told a trusted family member. For just a moment, I felt proud. However, a family member harshly responded saying, "Get the fuck out of my face!" The words hit me hard, leaving me feeling horrible and hurt. As I walked out of the room, tears filled my eyes. I concluded that nobody truly cared about me. This experience was traumatic. It was an attempt to use my voice, but I was met with harsh rejection and dismissal. In that moment, I made a vow to become self-sufficient. I was determined to show the world, my family, and especially my mother, that I could succeed on my own, without needing anyone's support.

These incidents ignited a strong drive within me to work hard, a determination to prove my worth that thrust me into adulthood prematurely. By the age of 12, I had mastered hairdressing, and by 15, I was already working in a salon. Stepping into the role of a provider, I took on the responsibility of ensuring that bills were paid, school supplies were purchased, and the needs of not only my immediate family but also my grandparents, extended family, and occasionally friends, were met. It was an immense responsibility for someone of my age, yet through perseverance and resilience, I managed to not only survive but also to thrive.

At 17, I accomplished what seemed impossible: I moved my mother into a better home, bought her a car, got new appliances for my grandparents, and managed to travel year after year to events like Freak-Nik, spring break, Circle City Classics, and Canada, paying for it all myself. Looking back, I am astonished by how much I achieved at such a young age.

I am thankful for always having a lot of "street smarts" and the ability to understand the reality of things.

Just as life seemed to be stabilizing in my teenage years, it took unexpected turns. At 19, I discovered a family secret that completely upended my understanding of my identity. I had always believed that Lloyd, the man I knew as my father, was not my biological dad. This shocking revelation made me question my very existence.

Rewinding to when I was 16, I met a distant cousin through mutual friends who insisted we meet, highlighting our similar mannerisms and ways of speaking. From 16 to 19, we grew incredibly close, hanging out daily, partying, sharing our thoughts, and traveling to different cities together. During this period, I lived more like an adult, shouldering high responsibilities and enjoying a corresponding level of freedom.

Fast forward to the age of 19. My biological father, Frank, learned about my close relationship with this distant cousin and became deeply concerned. Eventually, both our mothers revealed the truth: he was not my cousin, but my brother. This revelation came after a significant incident three months prior, when my mom abruptly asked me to stop visiting his house. Despite her request, our bond grew stronger—we were inseparable, like two peas in a pod. Then, one day, my mom sat me down for a startling conversation, asking, "What if your life wasn't what you thought it was?"

Me: "What if my life wasn't what I thought it was... What do you mean?"

Mom: "What if the life you are living is not the life you were supposed to live?"

Instantly, I knew something was up. Was my mother

about to tell me a secret? Something about me that only she knew. In my mind, I thought, is my mother not my mother? I immediately withdrew that thought because she had to be, or she would have given me back a long time ago. Then, a clear thought came into my spirit. "My dad is not my dad." She went on to tell me that my daddy wasn't who I thought he was. She told me that my daddy was the same man who had fathered the distant cousin I had been drawn to over the last three years.

Although my mom was reluctant, she revealed a secret to me, knowing I would eventually discover it. This disclosure added complexity to the narratives shaping my identity. Years of hurtful comments from my mother about my appearance had left me feeling ugly and rejected. Growing up, my bond with a distant cousin caused her discomfort to intensify. Her judgments about my relationships with men deepened my feelings of inadequacy and unworthiness. All these experiences stemmed from her projections and a deep-seated fear related to her secret.

Despite the tumultuous stories that defined my childhood and adolescence, I remained resilient and tenacious, determined to prove my worth to the world. My life was marked by a relentless pursuit of external validation, leading me into personal relationships where I continued to overextend myself to earn acceptance.

A couple of years after this experience, I went into a relationship with my kids' father. Now I realize that at that time in my life, I carried a lot of shame and had a negative self-view. And I found myself in a relationship that only amplified those emotions, where I kept working extra hard to prove myself. We had come from different backgrounds—his family was well-off, and my family was not. So, it was no surprise that his family questioned our relationship and my intentions, which made me work even harder to show them I was a good person and deserved to be with him.

After thirteen years together, my children's father and I had not married, and our relationship had become stifling. Deep-seated sorrow simmered within me, a hidden cost that remained invisible to those around me. I didn't grasp the extent of my emotional burdens until later.

After all the emotional and mental violations, I started to feel suffocated, like I was dying on the inside. My hard work and life overall had yielded great things, but I kept thinking, do others see me now? Does he see me? Unfortunately, nobody took the bait, not even him. I kept setting out more and more bait. In other words, I worked harder and harder to prove that I was worth marrying, that I was worth appreciating, that I was worth loving. Sadly, nothing happened other than I felt more and more invisible, bitter, and rejected. I started to feel used. I started to feel like nobody appreciated me. I had a feeling of intense sorrow deep inside. Nobody around me saw the emotional cost of all that was going on and all I was doing. I didn't see it either.

So many stories of betrayal, secrecy, pain, and violations made up my childhood and played a part in shaping my identity as I became an adult. Yet, it was through overcoming these tumultuous experiences that I learned the power of storytelling and its ability to define or redefine our lives. In the intricate web of stories that composed my life, one overarching narrative persisted: I was not enough. The underlying current was that I had to work ceaselessly to transcend this feeling. But the time had come to rewrite my story and affirm that I am enough, inherently deserving of love and acceptance. I recognized that I could choose to be the author of my own narrative, the leading lady in my life's story.

I realized that as a child, I was not unwanted; rather, I was a survivor of circumstances beyond my control. As an adult, my path had been forged through adversity, transforming me into a warrior who triumphed over adversity. My journey towards self-acceptance had just begun, but it was a path illuminated by the profound understanding that stories, whether they shackle us or set us free, are the threads that weave the tapestry of our lives. It was time to take hold of the pen and rewrite the narrative of my life. It was time to shed the shackles of self-doubt and shame and embrace the truth that I was enough just because I was me.

The Bible reminds us that the truth will set us free, and within that truth lies the profound realization that we are enough. Just like Dorothy in "The Wizard of Oz," who sought answers elsewhere only to find them within herself, we own the power to rewrite our stories.

There is an acronym for storytelling that I have found helpful both to myself and to others I have counseled. It is called the **ART** of life. It begins with Awareness, recognizing the roles we play in our own narratives. Are we victims of circumstance or authors of our destiny? **A**wareness empowers us to choose our response, rather than react to life's challenges.

R stands for Release and Retraining, liberating us from the constraints of old beliefs and behaviors. We learn new skills and perspectives, shedding the victim mindset.

T is for Tuning into a different frequency or elevated emotion and taking a different action. Tuning means choosing empowering narratives and our emotional responses. By consistently aligning our behaviors with a more positive storyline, we can rewrite the story of our lives.

We must be mindful of what we project into the world and remember that as an adult, no one else has the power to define us. Stepping into integrity and gratitude allows us to live in the present, rather than dragging and dwelling in the past, which we then perpetuate into our future.

Today, we have the opportunity to reframe our worth and validity. We are divine beings, unique and powerful. We have the ability to command every cell in our bodies to respond to our intentions. We are the captains of our ships, the directors of our movies, and the experts in our lives.

Our healing journey involves letting go of old stories and forgiving those who played a part in them, including ourselves. Compassion leads to forgiveness, setting us free to rewrite our narratives.

Know this: You are enough. Rewriting your story is not only possible but also deserved. Embrace the power of storytelling and become the author of your own destiny. You are a divine creation of life, deserving of love, acceptance, and a life lived to its fullest.

As I share these deeply personal experiences from my life, I do so not only to provide a window into my own journey but also to offer you valuable insights and tools for rewriting your own stories. The power of storytelling extends far beyond my own experiences; it's a universal force that shapes the human experience.

Recognizing the Stories We Carry

The first step in reshaping your narrative is recognizing the stories you carry with you. Take a moment to reflect on your life experiences, the narratives that have played on repeat in your mind, and the beliefs that may be holding you back. Are there stories of rejection, unworthiness, or inadequacy that have been etched into your consciousness? Identifying these narratives is the crucial starting point on the path to transformation.

Embrace Self-Compassion

It's easy to be hard on ourselves, especially when we've internalized negative stories. However, rewriting your narrative begins with self-compassion. Treat yourself with the same kindness, understanding, and forgiveness that you would offer to a dear friend facing similar challenges. Remember, it's okay to have flaws and imperfections; they make you uniquely human.

Seek Support and Connection

You don't have to embark on this journey alone. Seek out support from friends, family members, or a therapist or coach who can provide guidance, empathy, and a safe space to explore your stories. Connecting with others who have experienced similar struggles can be incredibly empowering and reassuring.

Reframe Your Beliefs

Challenge the stories that no longer serve you. Are they based on facts or assumptions? Are they holding you back from pursuing your dreams and goals? Start by reframing these beliefs with positive, empowering narratives. Replace "I'm not enough" with "I am resilient and capable." Shift "I am unwanted" to "I am deserving of love and acceptance."

Set Clear Intentions

As you rewrite your story, set clear intentions for the narrative you want to create. What do you want your life story to be? Define your values, aspirations, and the person you want to become. Align your actions and choices with these intentions, and allow them to guide you toward a brighter, more fulfilling future.

Practice Gratitude

Gratitude is a powerful tool for reshaping your story. Regularly acknowledge and appreciate the positive aspects of your life, no matter how small they may seem. Gratitude can help shift your focus away from negativity and towards the abundance and opportunities that surround you.

Patience and Persistence

Rewriting your story is a journey, not a destination. It requires patience and persistence. There may be moments of doubt or setbacks along the way, but remember that each step forward brings you closer to a narrative that empowers and uplifts you.

The Pen is in Your Hands

Ultimately, the pen is in your hands. You possess the power to redefine your story, to discard old narratives that hinder you, and to adopt an empowering new script. Your life is a canvas awaiting your creative imprint. As you read my journey, may it inspire and embolden you to commence the rewriting of your own tale.

In the upcoming chapters, we will dive deeper into the tools, exercises, and insights essential for your transformative journey. Together, we will explore the art of storytelling, resilience, self-discovery, and the limitless potential within each of us. Remember, you are the author of your own narrative, possessing both the ability and capacity to craft a story that resonates with authenticity, purpose, and fulfillment.

"Our mind is impressionable and powerful — it believes what it hears."

SHIELA LITTLE
@IAMSHAPINGSOLUTIONS

"Knowing and understanding our stories is key —shaping our stories is how we take the first step in breaking free from everything that holds us back in life."

SHIELA LITTLE
@IAMSHAPINGSOLUTIONS

"It is more important to live in the here and now, especially once you realize there is so much to be grateful for."

SHIELA LITTLE
@IAMSHAPINGSOLUTIONS

"Living from the past is just carrying stories over from the past which causes you to relive your yesterdays."

SHIELA LITTLE
@IAMSHAPINGSOLUTIONS

"We have the opportunity today to re-tell ourselves a new story about our worth, our validity, and who we are as children of The Most High."

SHIELA LITTLE
@IAMSHAPINGSOLUTIONS

2

STOP: UNVEILING TRIGGERS

I n the labyrinth of life's challenges and complexities, the STOP IT NOW framework, as revealed in this book, emerges as a guiding light. Its purpose? To provide you with the essential tools needed to halt the dis-eases that lead to destructive behaviors. These behaviors trap you, impeding your progress. They rob you of awareness—of being fully present and conscious, of seeing reality clearly, of acknowledging responsibility, recognizing your choices, and experiencing life free from the influence of others' perspectives. The STOP acronym serves as our compass, guiding us toward enhanced self-understanding. It enables us to rewrite our stories, reshape our narratives, and most importantly, reclaim control in our lives, leading to choices that are not only better but also healthier.

The "T" in STOP IT NOW, a focal point of this chapter, stands for Triggers. As defined by www.healthline.com, a trigger is "something that significantly affects your emotional state, often causing extreme overwhelm or distress. A trigger impacts your ability to remain present in the moment, bringing up specific thoughts and emotional patterns that can influence your behavior. Triggers vary widely and can be internal or external. Specific phrases, odors, or sounds, for example, can all be triggers for individuals who have experienced traumatic events."

For simplicity's sake within this book, let's define a traumatic event as any occurrence, regardless of its scale, that has the potential to induce significant stress on physical, emotional, spiritual, or psychological levels.

At the core of understanding triggers is the awareness of the stories we create within ourselves. Without awareness, we become prisoners of the past, our reality becomes distorted, and we unconsciously react to life based on past experiences. It is often said that if you continue responding to life in the same way you always have, the results will invariably remain the same.

This lack of awareness can lead to passive behaviors, and at times, passive-aggressive communication becomes our default approach. It's almost as if we have no other choice; we respond with sarcasm, opt for indirect communication, or simply shut down. The roots of such behaviors often lie in our paradigms, a concept that will be explored in depth in Chapter 4: Paradigms/Patterns. These paradigms, covered under the "P" in STOP IT NOW, act as the lens through which we perceive our reality and envision our future.

Triggers find their home in the shadows of the stories

we tell ourselves. Not recognizing these triggers can bind us, hindering our ability to curb behaviors that delay the realization of our desires. Unaware of our triggers, we become less effective, surrendering our power of choice to external influences. We communicate our needs inadequately, often responding to outdated events that may hold no relevance to our current situation. Caught in a trigger during an ongoing event, we forfeit the ability to express our true needs, becoming reactive rather than proactive in life's theater.

It's crucial to realize that life's experiences unfold in succession, each stirring a range of emotions, both positive and negative. Even joy can have its triggers. For instance, receiving a gift can fill your heart with gratitude, yet simultaneously trigger a belief that you must reciprocate. This internal dialogue, where you feel obliged to respond in kind, may not always align with your true desires, demonstrating how triggers can influence your actions.

Being aware of our triggers empowers us to control our responses. It allows us to step back and intentionally choose how to react to people and situations, rather than operating on autopilot. I experienced this when I was a hairstylist. If asked whether I could accommodate someone, my automatic response was always, "Of course!" This persisted even if it clashed with personal commitments or rest. This behavior, stemming from a fear of saying "no" and driven by concerns of being perceived as unkind, losing clients, or failing to meet expectations, often led me to say "yes" when I truly meant "no." Learning to say "no" to others and "yes" to myself was a pivotal step.

Another reason to be conscious of our triggers is that misunderstanding our responses in life can lead to recurring events with different actors and scenarios, perpetuating the same fears, heartaches, and feelings of inadequacy. Addressing these triggers can be transformative. Emotional Intelligence refers to these pivotal moments as "key moments," often rooted in childhood and reinforced during adolescence.

These key moments, forged in response to early experiences and shaped by our culture or environment, become our default reactions. As adults, faced with similar situations, we often revert to these ingrained patterns, trapping us in cycles of old behavior.

For instance, a key moment in my life revolved around the concept of leaving. My mother's dating experiences, ranging from amicable to emotionally tumultuous, often ended with us packing our bags and leaving, sometimes under distressing circumstances. This pattern, imprinted during my formative years, became my default response in my own relationships. Disagreements with boyfriends would lead me to declare the relationship over and leave, a learned response rather than a conscious choice. This pattern continued with my children's father, where arguments would lead to a temporary breakup, without ever addressing the underlying issues.

In my early thirties, I found myself repeating the same behavior—threatening to leave when arguments flared. I'd declare my intention to depart, leaving him to handle the children on his own. This pattern was a direct emulation of my mother's behavior. I continued this behavior in subsequent relationships, often packing my belongings and announcing my departure during arguments. One evening, after a familiar scene unfolded, I realized I was mirroring my mother's actions over the years. I was following the same pattern for dealing with anger. Instead of leaving, I decided to retreat to my room, seeking solace behind closed doors to regain my composure. I gradually learned to change my approach, becoming more aware, present, and attuned to reality. I began to recognize that I had choices beyond escape. This shift marked a significant change for me. It was an acknowledgment that I wasn't limited to escaping situations when triggered by anger. I could communicate my feelings and express my hurt or disappointment.

In truth, anger often masks underlying deeper secondary emotions like frustration and irritation. These secondary emotions are triggered by the thoughts we have about the emotion we are experiencing. Throughout the years, when I'd respond with anger, I was often masking the feelings of hurt and frustration that arose from unmet expectations. Recognizing this helped me understand that leaving during moments of anger wasn't the most constructive response. Instead, I needed to communicate my emotions and express what triggered them. This shift was in stark contrast to my previous modus operandi, where I'd temporarily flee a situation only to return to the same unresolved circumstances, leading to recurring chaos and disappointment.

My children's father and I remained together for thirteen years, and throughout that time, we perpetuated the same pattern of behavior. There was an instance when I deviated from our usual routine, yet this change didn't resolve our issues because we continued to avoid communication. I had to confront the root of my triggers and the key moments that birthed them. This led me to the revelation that my adult relationships were merely amplifying preexisting emotional wounds. It was clear that this cycle would persist unless I chose to STOP IT NOW. I began the journey of healing those wounds, learning to communicate my needs and understand my triggers in a healthier manner.

Triggers are never without meaning or the stories we associate with them. They shape the lenses through which we view life and the paradigms that guide our actions. For instance, my reactions of suspicion and reactivity were rooted in a lens of fear. This paradigm, fueled by feelings of powerlessness and lack of control, convinced me that change was unattainable. As a result, I tended to react impulsively rather than respond thoughtfully, blame others instead of accepting responsibility, and seek escape instead of confronting my challenges. It was only by shifting from a fear-based paradigm (victimhood) to one of integrity (empowerment) that I began making autonomous choices, rather than yielding to societal pressures or perceived obligations. This shift allowed me to trust situations, stay mindful of my decisions, embrace intimacy and vulnerability, and importantly, make choices based on my own needs and values, rather than bending to others' expectations. (We will explore paradigms and patterns further in Chapter 4)

When triggers arise, they bring with them significant meanings and stories, shaped by ongoing events and our perspectives. These events and their physical sensations might resonate with past experiences, but awareness opens the door to transformation. In my journey, I observed that in triggering situations, I often held my breath, a realization that dawned on me during meditation practice. This awareness led me to consciously remind myself to breathe in such moments. Another sign of awareness was recognizing physical signs, like muscle tension. To break the cycle of a trigger, it's crucial to understand the emotions it evokes, the narratives you attach to it, and the physical sensations it triggers. Reflect on the emotions each situation brings. Do you feel inadequate, hurt, sad, helpless, or angry? How do you typically react when triggered?

Triggers inherently assign meaning and stories to events, significantly influenced by previous events or our perspective. In our interactions, whether they involve conflict, success, relationships, failure, judgments, or others' opinions, it's vital to examine our reactions.

This self-awareness enables us to consciously choose new ways of engaging with current experiences. In my case, rather than continuing arguments with my partner, I sought solitude, processed my emotions, and then communicated them clearly. Such awareness enhances our decision-making and frees us from the constraints of counterproductive patterns.

Paradoxically, success can trigger anxiety. In my experience, whenever I was on the cusp of success or faced opportunities for financial growth, anxiety would emerge, often leading to self-sabotage. I found myself hesitating to fully engage or show up. This behavior was rooted in my previous understanding of money and success.

A notable example was when I hesitated at the prospect of a promising contract. This hesitation forced me to examine my beliefs about money and success. At that moment, I recognized that the opportunity was triggering doubts about my abilities. However, I began to reframe my definition of success, seeing it as a multi-dimensional concept. I realized success wasn't just about financial gains; it also meant cultivating loving, intimate, and mutually respectful relationships, personal growth, a sense of purpose, and the ability to positively influence others. Learning to love every aspect of myself and embracing my life, I redefined success, which helped me regain control.

When another contract opportunity came along, it initially triggered anxiety. Yet, when it didn't work out, I didn't view it as rejection, but simply as an occurrence. Had I not shifted my perspective, I might have fallen into self-doubt and insecurity. Instead, this incident became a pivotal moment, opening new paths and empowering me to choose my responses to similar future situations.

Remember, triggers often conceal narratives and meanings that are not influenced by the specific situation and your viewpoint at the time. However, with increased self-awareness, you can alter your responses. Be attentive to your feelings, behaviors, and actions when triggered. This awareness is key to personal growth and transformation, steering you towards the life you truly desire and deserve. Your reaction can have profound effects, either strengthening or undermining you.

In each triggering circumstance, I learned to ask myself questions like:

- What emotions am I experiencing right now?
- What stories or beliefs are associated with these emotions?
- What is my usual response pattern when triggered?
- Is this response pattern aligned with my true desires and goals?

These questions enabled me to pause and reflect, leading to a shift from reaction to response. I began making conscious choices that aligned with my authentic self, gradually rewriting my story.

Shaping Your Story

As we conclude this chapter on triggers, it's essential to leave you with some insights and tools to aid in rewriting your story. Triggers are not your enemies; they are your messengers. They bring to light the parts of your narrative that require your attention. To rewrite your story, follow these steps:

- **Self-Reflection:** Start by identifying your triggers. Reflect on situations or events that consistently provoke strong emotional reactions in you. Be honest with yourself about your emotional responses.
- **Embrace Awareness:** Recognize that triggers are a natural part of life. Embrace them with curiosity rather than fear or resistance. The more aware you become of your triggers, the more power you have to change your responses.
- **Explore the Stories:** Dive into the stories and beliefs associated with your triggers. What narratives have you created around these triggers? How do these stories influence your behavior and decisions?
- **Practice Pause:** When triggered, practice pausing before reacting. Take a deep breath and ask yourself the four questions mentioned earlier. This pause

will create a space for you to choose your response consciously.

- **Choose Empowerment:** Make choices aligning with your authentic self and desired outcomes. Be proactive in rewriting your story by responding to triggers to serve your growth and well-being.
- **Seek Support:** If your triggers are deeply rooted and challenging to navigate alone, consider seeking support from a therapist, counselor, or support group. They can provide guidance and tools for healing and transformation.
- **Patience and Persistence:** Rewriting your story is a journey that requires patience and persistence. Be kind to yourself as you work through your triggers, and remember that change takes time.

Remember, your story is not set in stone. You have the power to rewrite it, to create a narrative that aligns with your true self and leads to a more fulfilling life. In the upcoming chapters, we'll delve deeper into the STOP IT NOW framework, exploring each element to help you on your journey of personal transformation and self-empowerment.

"We lack awareness of the stories we tell ourselves and how those stories trigger us."

SHIELA LITTLE
@IAMSHAPINGSOLUTIONS

If you respond to life the same way you have always responded to life, the results will be the same."

SHIELA LITTLE
@IAMSHAPINGSOLUTIONS

"Awareness can help you make better choices and stop repeating broken, unsuccessful behavior patterns."

SHIELA LITTLE
@IAMSHAPINGSOLUTIONS

"The truth is that to have something different, you must do something different. You must inject new experiences and narratives to have a different outcome."

SHIELA LITTLE
@IAMSHAPINGSOLUTIONS

3

STOP: OPPORTUNITY COST - EMBRACING LIFE'S CHOICES

As we embark on our journey of personal transformation through life, we inevitably encounter a concept frequently used in business – opportunity cost. In this book and under the STOP IT NOW framework, opportunity cost is defined as the values, benefits, beliefs, or habits we give up in favor of something we perceive as more valuable or beneficial. As we strive to reshape our lives, opportunities will constantly arise, but choosing to seize them or not involves an opportunity cost. The idea here is that you must be willing to relinquish certain things or people for the sake of your well-being and a future filled with health and fulfillment.

Life's decisions are inherently intertwined with emotions. Feelings like guilt, shame, confusion, and doubt often accompany our choices, leading us to ponder questions like "What if?" or "Should I?" when facing decisions or reflecting on deferred ones. Delving deeper, we may wonder, "What if I had done this instead?" or lament, "I wish I had done that." This introspection is at the heart of understanding opportunity cost. Many people fail to live the lives they truly desire and deserve because of these costs. When you cling to a particular narrative, it's crucial to acknowledge the real price you're paying, including both the consequences and benefits of your decisions.

For instance, I used to find myself contemplating what might have happened if I had ended a relationship with my children's father earlier, recognizing the signs of our unhealthy dynamic. Where would I be now? Would I be a single mother, perhaps leading a different, less stressful life?

The stories we tell ourselves trigger emotions and guide our choices. These narratives often foster limiting beliefs, leading us to ponder what might be different or how life could look if we made a change or stayed the course. Such questions can leave us feeling despondent, defeated, resentful, and trapped in the past, in a world of "should haves," "could haves," and "would haves."

In the case of my children's father, I remained in the relationship because, at the time, I saw only one viable option. The narrative in my head made leaving seem unfeasible, as I feared navigating life alone, raising my boys in a single-parent household, relying on a single income, and potentially jeopardizing my emotional well-being. I wasn't prepared to pay that price. However, over time, I realized that I was convincing myself to stay and do what

I thought was right. Yet, as the relationship progressed, I learned that what seemed right for me might not be the best for everyone else. I had to change my narrative and face the costs, even if it meant confronting my fears and avoidances. Choosing a different path meant an unforeseen life for myself, my partner, and my children. I opted for a path of empowerment; despite the initial challenges, the journey was ultimately rewarding.

I once dated a man, knowing from the start that he wasn't going to be a part of my long-term future. Early on, I recognized our attachment as unhealthy, yet he seemed to tick all the right boxes. We shared a satisfying physical and intimate relationship and collaborated well in business. However, he lacked honesty. About a year into our relationship, while out with him, I unexpectedly ran into an old friend. This encounter stirred a surge of positive emotions within me. My old friend, perceiving the mismatch in my current relationship, questioned why I was with my current partner. He possessed qualities I admired and attributes I yearned for in a relationship.

This reconnection with my old friend sparked a whirlwind of emotions. He lived out of town, which I thought made it easier to maintain this secret connection discreetly. We planned a meeting, and I even drove an hour to his house. But upon arrival, I found myself sitting in my car in his driveway, unable to go inside. I took a picture of his house and later sent it to him, avoiding his calls all night. The next day, I explained my reluctance to meet.

I convinced myself that the uncertainties surrounding this old friend were too significant. I began to doubt, wondering if he could be the catalyst for leaving my current situation. The thought of revealing this secret encounter to my current partner loomed over me. Ultimately, I chose not to pursue things with my old friend, fearing the potential consequences and costs of choosing him over my current partner, with whom I had a functional relationship.

Deep down, I didn't want to upset the person I was with, despite knowing that our relationship was faltering. My loyalty stayed with him; I didn't want him to perceive me as someone who would abandon ship during tough times. Once again, I found myself committed to a dynamic where my needs were unmet, leading to growing dissatisfaction.

Later, I realized that my fear was more than just fear of the unknown; I was apprehensive about stepping into uncharted territory. Despite our meaningful connection, I questioned the worth of a new experience with my old friend. Our communication eventually ceased, as it seemed we were heading nowhere. A month later, my partner and I parted ways. It was then that I acknowledged to myself that I had endured enough. I had tolerated the unhealthy dynamics of intimate relationships for so long that I could no longer bear it.

This breakup was delayed because I had emotionally shut down, becoming numb to my own needs. The relationship was a profound lesson, but after it ended, I often found myself reflecting on the person I had let go. Ultimately, I ended up with neither of them. I felt disappointed in myself, believing I had missed the chance to explore something different, to start anew with the possibility of a healthier dynamic – or so I told myself.

The overarching theme of this story is my awareness of what I had in my relationship, and while there was some value in it, I tolerated aspects that were detrimental to my emotional well-being. I realized I had a window of opportunity but didn't seize it due to my unwillingness to pay the "opportunity cost" of that decision.

However, I am grateful for ending the pattern of unhealthy dynamics, as continuing would have trapped me in a turbulent and drama-filled situation, leading to a messy, regrettable ordeal. I'm thankful that my old friend reentered my life, showing me a different path and helping me recognize what I truly desired in a partner.

Several months later, I had a chance to go on a date with my old friend again, but nothing substantial developed. The damage had already been done. However, this experience left me with a wealth of aspirations and dreams for future relationships. In the end, I neither pursued a new beginning nor stayed with my previous partner. This story underscores the importance of recognizing the stories we tell ourselves and understanding their associated costs.

Understanding these narratives and their costs is crucial.

When life presents us with a crossroads, we must discern whether there's a hint of divine guidance. Life continually offers opportunities, some we request and others that surprise us. It's vital to remember that things may not always unfold as we expect or desire. Therefore, we must stay open and attentive to what truly aligns with our essence. Deep within, our genuine path awaits discovery. In my case, fear held me back from embracing the opportunity cost. It was rooted in my fears of commitment, change, abandonment, and the unknown. As I moved forward, I learned to trust myself more, realizing the potential for engaging in healthy dynamics and embracing new possibilities.

After dedicating significant effort to personal growth, I gained a profound understanding of the myriad opportunity costs I had avoided throughout my life due to feelings of unworthiness. My hesitation in making pivotal decisions led to substantial emotional, financial, and physical repercussions. However, the silver lining is that each of these experiences taught me valuable lessons. Today, I am proud to say that I remain present, savoring each moment and recognizing its value in my life. I have come to understand the importance of making decisions and how those choices, or the lack thereof, shape my future.

Opportunity costs are challenging decisions that we must confront to achieve the lives we desire and deserve. These choices may require us to disappoint others, evoke uncomfortable emotions, and sometimes appear selfish or unreasonable. Nevertheless, you are either in control of your life's decisions, or you are allowing someone else to make them for you. Often, we avoid taking responsibility for our lives, playing the role of the victim and blaming our circumstances on external factors. In truth, we either contributed to our current situation, participated in the choices that led us here, or let people, careers, children, or external circumstances dictate our path. However, you have the power to take control and steer your life in the direction you desire, one decision at a time. This approach might be new to you, but deep inside, you know that something must change, something must STOP. Yes, change carries a cost, and though it may initially seem overwhelming, unjust, or unsettling, the opportunities it creates will ultimately prove to be a valuable investment.

Now, let's add some insights and guidance to help you understand and apply the concept of opportunity cost:

Insights and Applications for You

As you reflect on the concept of opportunity cost in your own life, remember that understanding and embracing it can be a transformative journey. Here are some key takeaways to consider:

1. **Embrace Self-Reflection**: Just as I've shared my personal experiences, take the time to reflect on your own life. Identify moments when you faced critical

choices and consider what you gained and lost with each decision. And remember, not deciding is a decision.

2. **Recognize Your Narrative:** Your life is shaped by the stories you tell yourself. Acknowledge the narratives that influence your decisions and evaluate their actual costs. Sometimes, the fear of the unknown or the weight of societal expectations can prevent you from embracing opportunities for change and growth.

3. **Acknowledge Fear and Change:** Fear often stands as the sentinel guarding the gateway to opportunity. Whether it's the fear of commitment, change, or the unknown, acknowledge these fears. Sometimes, confronting them head-on can lead to profound growth.

4. **Value Your Worth:** Understand that you are inherently worthy of a life filled with joy, fulfillment, and love. Don't let fear or external influences devalue your worth. Prioritize your well-being.

5. **Empower Yourself:** Realize that you have the agency to make choices in your life. You can steer your own ship. It may require courage and sacrifice, but the rewards are worth it.

6. **Take Responsibility:** Avoid the victim mentality. Recognize that as an adult, your choices, or lack thereof, have led you to where you are today. Take responsibility for your life's direction and be proactive

in making decisions that align with your true desires and values.

7. **Trust Your Inner Guidance:** When faced with life's crossroads, pay attention to your intuition. Trust that deep down, you know what is right for you. Be open to unexpected opportunities, even if they don't align with your initial expectations. Fear can be a powerful deterrent, but self-trust can guide you toward a more fulfilling future.

8. **Embrace Your Power of Choice:** Take responsibility for your life's direction. Understand that you are the driver of your own journey, and your choices shape your path. Don't let external circumstances or the decisions of others define your destiny. Embrace the costs and rewards of your decisions, for they are the stepping stones to the life you desire and deserve.

9. **Welcome Change:** Embrace change as a necessary part of growth. Remember that it might not always appear in the way you expect, but it often leads to unforeseen opportunities and personal evolution.

10. **Invest in Your Future:** Understand that the opportunity cost may involve temporary discomfort, unsettling emotions, or even disappointing others. However, the investments you make in yourself and your future can lead to a life that truly fulfills you.

As you progress through this book, keep these insights in mind. Opportunity cost is not just a concept to grasp intellectually; it's a principle to integrate into your life. Embrace the changes, confront your fears, and remember that every decision you make shapes your future. You have the power to STOP and steer your life in the direction of your dreams.

"In life, we must make decisions, and with those choices come emotions. So don't allow your feelings about external circumstances or the opinions of others to define your destiny. "

SHIELA LITTLE
@IAMSHAPINGSOLUTIONS

"Life constantly presents us with opportunities, things we ask for and don't expect."

SHIELA LITTLE
@IAMSHAPINGSOLUTIONS

"Opportunity costs are challenging decisions we must make to move towards the life we desire and deserve."

SHIELA LITTLE
@IAMSHAPINGSOLUTIONS

"With change comes a cost, and although these costs may bring dis-ease, the opportunity they will provide you will be worth your investment."

SHIELA LITTLE
@IAMSHAPINGSOLUTIONS

"Learn how to embrace the costs and rewards of your decisions, for they are the stepping stones to create the life you desire and deserve."

SHIELA LITTLE
@IAMSHAPINGSOLUTIONS

4

STOP: UNDERSTANDING YOUR PARADIGMS AND PATTERNS

I n my role as a therapist, coach, and professional development guide, I often share an analogy that reflects the essence of life. Picture yourself seated at a dining room table. Most dining room tables feature a centerpiece that varies in appearance depending on where you choose to sit. Just as in life, diverse perspectives or "stories" emerge depending on your point of view. These perspectives are what we call paradigms. Paradigms, in essence, are the mental filters or images that shape our interpretation of life's experiences.

Now, let's revisit that dining room table. Envision your favorite seat; for me, it's the head of the table. In this spot, my view of the centerpiece remains constant. But if I choose to sit elsewhere, say, on the side, my perspective changes. Suddenly, I might not see the prominent red rose with a few of its petals gently stained, and I begin searching for it. This mirrors our life journey. When we do not perceive something as familiar, be it a behavior or belief we're accustomed to, we instinctively hunt for it. This process of seeking the familiar leads to the development of patterns. Why? Because we don't view the world as an objective reality; instead, we perceive it through the lens of our beliefs. In simpler terms, we look at any given situation through the filter of our own core beliefs. This is precisely why understanding your paradigms is of paramount importance. In the realm of emotional intelligence, four distinct paradigms come to the forefront:

- **Fear**: A paradigm marked by reactivity, victim, and blame, a mindset anchored in "having to" do something.
- **Duty**: This paradigm is all about conforming to stereotypes and societal expectations, embodying the "should do" mindset.
- **Achievement**: A goal-oriented, independent paradigm where the guiding principle is "ought to."
- **Integrity**: Here, you find consciousness, alignment, and interdependence, a mindset rooted in "choosing to."

Each paradigm through which you view the world lays the foundation for the patterns in your life. The way you perceive the world profoundly influences your self-concept and concepts about the world and becomes the bedrock upon which your habits and beliefs are constructed. While some habits and beliefs are imposed upon us, we also actively form habits and beliefs based on societal norms and personal experiences. These habits and beliefs soon become integral to our identity, weaving themselves into our life stories.

Consider the habit of wearing makeup. From a young age, I was often told by peers and older women that makeup becomes essential as you age. I was a tomboy, content with just Vaseline on my lips. However, as I grew older, applying concealer daily evolved from a simple task to a ritual, and eventually, a habit. Soon, stepping out without concealer felt uncomfortable, signaling a shift in my self-image and worldview.

In my book, "STOP IT NOW," I aim to empower readers to recognize and transform life stories, habits, and beliefs that no longer contribute positively to their well-being. It's crucial to not only understand the narrative you've created for yourself but also to recognize the underlying paradigm shaping your perspective of the world.

My sense of safety, or lack thereof, significantly influenced my adherence to a fear-based mindset throughout my twenties. I subconsciously found solace in submissiveness and adopting a victim role, reinforcing my belief in my inadequacy and life's constant struggles. I viewed the world as a hostile place, where trust was scarce and everyone seemed like an adversary. Seeking an escape, I immersed myself in academia and work, engaging in a relentless cycle of study, work, board commitments, and community projects.

Despite my accomplishments on paper, I felt isolated and disconnected.

Life's pivotal moments often shape our paradigms and define our life stories. For me, a profound sense of disconnection from my family and feeling unwanted were such moments. These feelings led to an overpowering need to overcompensate, a tendency that persisted into adulthood. Carrying the belief of being undesired, I embraced the duty paradigm. I believed that relentless hard work and support for others would earn me acceptance. Yet, acceptance remained out of reach, leaving me battling feelings of neglect and inadequacy. My firm belief in my insufficiency drove me to constantly pursue what I thought I "should do" to alter my circumstances.

My perspectives on men were also shaped by these paradigms. Despite being a therapist advocating for healthy relationships, I found myself distrusting men in my personal life. I viewed them with suspicion, seeing them as untrustworthy and driven by base desires. This fear made me question the point of engaging in relationships with seemingly predictable, disappointing outcomes.

Realizing this, I chose to break free from this cycle. I couldn't continue on a path leading only to pain. Transitioning from fear and duty to an achievement paradigm, I started making decisions based on my desires, not others' expectations. This shift was met with accusations of selfishness from those around me.

My relationship with my children's father transformed too. I aimed for a healthier co-parenting dynamic, confronting the duty paradigm directly. I needed to protect myself and stop being perpetually obliging. I mistook rigid control and boundaries for safety, viewing relationships as inherently unsafe.

It's essential to understand that duty is not fear, nor an escape from life. Duty involves responsibility driven by external expectations, often to gain approval. If you find yourself enduring situations for others' favor, you're likely operating within the duty paradigm. It means staying silent, constantly striving to meet others' expectations, and neglecting your own desires.

Before my transformative journey, I was deeply entrenched in the duty paradigm. I juggled multiple roles – breadwinner, mother, professional, volunteer, and friend – all while exhaustively striving to maintain an appearance of success. Success was measured by an unending checklist of achievements. Yet, despite external accolades, I felt a profound emptiness within. After achieving a goal, earning a degree, or being recognized, I denied myself the satisfaction of feeling accomplished. Instead, I quickly moved on to the next objective, perpetually trapped on life's hamster wheel. Stress took its toll, leading to chronic daily headaches. I relied on daily medications that only induced drowsiness, leaving me feeling inadequate.

The relentless grind became unsustainable. Living

paycheck to paycheck, with no breathing room, my mind raced at night, robbing me of sleep. Overwhelmed, I decided to break this ceaseless cycle. Transitioning from the fear and duty paradigms to the achievement paradigm was significant but only a stepping stone. I adopted a "selfish" mindset, often misunderstood by those who couldn't grasp my new focus.

My approach to relationships changed drastically. I began dating others, prompting my ex to claim I was more invested in other relationships than in ours. He was partly right—I was drawn to relationships where my interests were reciprocated. I embarked on a journey to live authentically, co-creating experiences with others instead of waiting to be seen and provided for.

The "P" in STOP IT NOW plays a crucial role in this journey toward emotional intelligence. The goal is not to linger in fear and duty but to transition to the achievement paradigm, where genuine transformation begins. Here, you decide to conquer life, being true to yourself and recognizing that growth requires embracing your unique essence. You understand that focusing on yourself first is necessary for your circumstances to change.

A pivotal moment in my journey was ending my relationship with my children's father. Both my mother and grandmother questioned my decision. He had commendable qualities, they argued, but my inner turmoil persisted. I refused to sacrifice my peace and intimacy for a semblance of a relationship. I yearned to give not out of obligation but from genuine want. I sought authenticity over external validation. I was no longer willing to adhere to the admirable qualities of someone else that I had yet to realize in myself. An inner yearning pushed me forward, urging me to break free from my constraints. I needed to be selfish long enough, acknowledge myself long enough, and outgrow that phase long enough before returning to a place of genuine care and concern for others. This marked my transition into the paradigm of integrity, the antithesis of fear.

Integrity is the mindset where you embrace and align with your higher being, your purposeful self, with confidence that all events will ultimately serve your greater good. In this mindset, you see others as fellow beings deserving of the same compassion you desire. If I dedicate 16 hours a day to helping a friend with her business while living in the paradigm of integrity, it's because I choose to do so. Similarly, if I accept less than par in a person, it is a conscious choice.

Integrity embodies vulnerability, where trust in others coexists with the absence of people-pleasing. Life is perceived as a journey, not a destination. You seek to stay present in life's unfolding moments, accepting the good, the bad, and the indifferent. In this state, you recognize and embrace your true self and your interconnectedness with others, positioned to serve others without depleting yourself.

Patterns play a significant role in this journey. Energy never disappears; it merely transforms. In the fear paradigm, you may see everyone as a potential adversary, always on guard. Duty can lead to patterns of overextension, saying "yes" to everything, and enduring immense stress. The achievement paradigm might make you self-absorbed and egotistic. These are all transcended in the actual transformation that occurs when you break these patterns and shift to the integrity paradigm. Here, you align with your authentic self and with others, attract experiences that resonate with your core, step away from self-sabotage, and embrace a life of service.

Take a moment to consider if you hold onto patterns founded on limiting beliefs. Awareness of your paradigms is crucial for advancement. Procrastination often signals a lack of awareness, a stagnation in the initial paradigms, thwarting your desires. Duty may appear empowering on the surface, but it ultimately undermines your pursuit of unconditional love. Yearning for unconditional love while mired in duty indicates you're not living as your highest self, making true acceptance elusive.

Understanding the lens through which you perceive life is paramount. Consider changing your seat at the table to one that offers a clearer view of your paradigms. Recognize the roles you play – victim (fear paradigm), savior (duty paradigm), villain (achievement paradigm) – and empower yourself to shed these unhealthy lenses. Change can be uncomfortable and challenging, but it is profoundly rewarding. Authentic transformation unfolds from within.

The STOP Process

The "STOP" section of the framework marks the initial phase of your journey toward becoming your healthiest self. It's a pattern of behaviors that begins with self-awareness. Personal change involves several unique steps. Often, people think of the change or goal they want and dive directly into it, only to find themselves back where they started. The STOP IT NOW framework focuses on "doing" less to "become" more, a different approach compared to traditional models.

First, become aware of the patterns hidden within the story you tell yourself about the goal or life you intend to experience. STOP and let go of the old patterns, beliefs, and stories. To assist in this stage, acknowledge your feelings, journal, and communicate to yourself the reasons these patterns, beliefs, and stories exist and the benefits of letting them go. Identify the exact behaviors, thoughts, and beliefs you are stopping that keep you stuck. Then recognize the opportunity cost of these patterns and understand the lens through which you perceive the world.

Next, you want to neutralize – the "IT" in "STOP IT NOW." This step is challenging yet necessary. It involves refraining from reverting to old behaviors, maintaining neutrality, and intentionally avoiding judgment from your inner critic while priming your mind with your life vision. Focus and meditate on your goal, your "why." This fosters internal change that will eventually extend into your experiences. Eventually, new behaviors, patterns, and beliefs start to take shape. First, we make our habits, and then our habits make us.

New behaviors, even if uncomfortable and challenging, are where fundamental transformation occurs. Learn to manage emotions during this transition. First, stop and become aware of hidden patterns, understand their opportunity costs, and recognize your lens. Then, engage in a new pattern, venture, or relationship to see if you've genuinely stopped the old one. The next step is to stop judging the old behaviors. This neutrality fosters internal change, which, in turn, radiates outward to your friends, family, and community.

The STOP process can be difficult, but once you're genuinely aware of what needs to stop, confront the associated emotions, and take the right action, change happens. Therapy and coaching encourage this kind of thinking, enabling you to see things as they truly are, unearth limiting beliefs, and shift into a paradigm of integrity. In this paradigm, you attract experiences congruent with your true self, not just what you want, but who you genuinely are. Your actions reflect your core values, and you seek to be of service without self-sabotage.

In conclusion, recognizing your paradigms and patterns is a critical step on your journey to self-discovery and personal development. Understand that both internal and external change is a necessary part of this process. Although it might be uncomfortable, it is precisely in this discomfort where fundamental transformation begins. By adopting a paradigm of integrity, you embrace your true self, paving the way to a healthier and happier life.

Addressing Old Patterns and Updating Your Paradigm

Now that we've delved into the world of paradigms and patterns, you might wonder how you can apply this knowledge to your life for personal growth and transformation. The journey to self-improvement starts with self-awareness and conscious choices. Here are some steps you can take to address old patterns and update your paradigm:

1. **Self-Reflection:** Begin by taking a good look at your life and the recurring patterns that may be holding you back. Are there aspects of your life where you feel stuck or unfulfilled? Identifying these patterns is the first step toward change.

2. **Identify Your Paradigms**: Explore the paradigms through which you view the world. Are you primarily operating from a place of fear, duty, achievement, or integrity? Recognize that these paradigms shape your beliefs and actions.

3. **Recognize Trigger Moments**: Think back to pivotal moments in your life that may have contributed to the formation of your paradigms. Understanding the

origins of these beliefs can help you make sense of your current patterns.

4. **Challenge Your Beliefs**: Ask yourself if your existing beliefs and patterns serve your best interests. Are they helping you lead a fulfilling life or holding you back? Be open to challenging and questioning your beliefs.

5. **Embrace Change:** Understand that change can be uncomfortable, but it's often necessary for personal growth. Moving from one paradigm to another may require breaking old habits and stepping out of your comfort zone.

6. **Seek Support:** It's beneficial to seek guidance from a therapist, coach, or mentor. These professionals can assist you in navigating the process of updating your paradigm and breaking free from limiting patterns.

7. **Practice Mindfulness:** Engaging in mindfulness meditation and self-awareness exercises can be immensely beneficial. These practices help you stay present and observe your thoughts and behaviors objectively, enabling you to make conscious choices that are aligned with your desired paradigm.

8. **Set Clear Intentions:** Define the paradigm you want to operate from and set clear intentions for the changes you want to make in your life. Write down your goals and aspirations.

9. **Take Small Steps:** Transformation doesn't happen overnight. Start with small, manageable steps toward

updating your paradigm and breaking free from old patterns. Celebrate your progress along the way.

10. **Stay Committed:** Be patient and stay committed to your personal development journey. There may be setbacks, but remember that each step forward is a step closer to living a life that aligns with your true self.

Updating your paradigm and addressing old patterns is a continuous journey. Embrace this process as an opportunity to gain valuable experience, evolve, and create a life that truly reflects your authentic self. Your journey towards personal development and transformation begins with the awareness that change is within your reach. So, take that first step, and remember that you have the power to shape your own life.

In the next chapter, we'll delve into the "IT" in our STOP IT NOW framework, focusing on the concept of "Integrating the IT Factor" and how it can lead you to a more balanced and harmonious life. Stay committed to your journey of self-discovery and personal growth. Within this journey lies the key to creating the life you truly desire and deserve.

"We don't see the world as it is; instead, we perceive it through the lens of our core beliefs."

SHIELA LITTLE
@IAMSHAPINGSOLUTIONS

"True
transformation
occurs when you
break the
patterns and shift
to the paradigm
that allows you to
align with your
authentic self and
accept others for
who they are."

SHIELA LITTLE
@IAMSHAPINGSOLUTIONS

"Change may be uncomfortable and challenging, but it's profoundly rewarding. Authentic transformation unfolds from within.

SHIELA LITTLE
@IAMSHAPINGSOLUTIONS

"To move towards the next level in life, you must get selfish long enough to get what you need."

SHIELA LITTLE
@IAMSHAPINGSOLUTIONS

5

STOP IT: "CONCURRING THE IT FACTOR: TRANSFORMING YOUR INNER LANDSCAPE"

I n this pivotal chapter, we embark on a profound journey into the depths of our inner world, focusing on the transformative power of integrating the inner critic and self-talk, which we'll refer to as the "IT" Factor. While the initial part of this book, "STOP," focused on the external aspects of our lives, we now pivot inward, beginning with the realm of inner dialog. Our inner dialog is a potent force, wielding incredible influence over our thoughts and actions.

The terms "inner critic" and "self-talk" both refer to aspects of our internal thought processes. However, they carry different connotations and implications:

Inner Critic: The inner critic is a specific aspect of self-talk characterized by negative or critical thoughts directed towards oneself. It often involves self-judgment, self-doubt, and a tendency to focus on perceived flaws or shortcomings.

The inner critic can be quite harsh and unrelenting,

frequently leading to feelings of inadequacy, low self-esteem, and anxiety. This aspect of our thought process is often more focused on evaluating and critiquing ourselves in a negative light, rather than offering constructive feedback.

Self-Talk: Self-talk is a broader term that encompasses all the internal dialogue and thoughts that we have throughout the day. This includes both positive and negative thoughts. Self-talk can be either constructive or destructive. Constructive self-talk involves positive affirmations, motivation, and encouragement. Destructive self-talk includes negative thoughts, self-criticism, and self-doubt. Self-talk is fundamental to our mental processes and can greatly influence our emotions, behaviors, and decision-making.

The primary distinction is that the "inner critic" refers specifically to the negative, self-critical aspect of self-talk, whereas "self-talk" encompasses the entire spectrum of internal dialogue, including both positive and negative elements. It's vital to be aware of our self-talk, as it significantly impacts our mental and emotional well-being. Recognizing and challenging the inner critic is a crucial step towards fostering a more positive and self-affirming inner dialogue.

Our belief system plays a significant role in shaping our self-talk and its interaction with our inner critic. Here's how they influence each other:

Belief System and Self-Talk: Our belief system comprises the core beliefs, values, and assumptions we hold about ourselves, others, and the world. These beliefs, whether conscious or subconscious, are formed through experiences, upbringing, culture, and personal reflection. Our belief system strongly influences our self-talk. For instance, if someone harbors a belief of being inherently unworthy or incapable, their self-talk is likely dominated by negative, self-critical thoughts that reinforce this belief. Conversely, a belief in one's abilities and self-worth can lead to more positive and self-affirming self-talk.

Belief System and Inner Critic: The inner critic often operates based on our underlying beliefs about ourselves. If we have deep-seated negative beliefs about our worth or capabilities, the inner critic tends to amplify and reinforce these beliefs through self-critical thoughts. For example, someone who believes they are fundamentally flawed may find their inner critic constantly highlighting their perceived shortcomings, reinforcing this negative belief.

Feedback Loop: There exists a feedback loop between our belief system, self-talk, and inner critic. Negative beliefs can fuel the inner critic, leading to a cycle of self-criticism and reinforced negative beliefs. On the flip side, positive beliefs can result in more positive self-talk, which can mitigate the influence of the inner critic.

As the Bible insightfully states, "All happens in spirit (energy) before it happens in the material world." Beliefs are the offspring of our energy and the whispers of our souls. They manifest as thoughts and shape our perception of the world, often taking root in our minds during childhood—a critical period for brain development. These beliefs form the bedrock of our lives, serving as the lens through which we interpret reality.

Our belief system acts as the framework guiding our self-talk and inner critic. Negative or unhelpful beliefs can fuel a harsh inner critic and destructive self-talk, while positive and affirming beliefs can lead to more constructive self-talk and a gentler inner dialogue. Recognizing and actively shifting negative beliefs toward more positive and realistic ones can significantly foster a healthier inner dialogue.

Understanding our own beliefs is a complex and challenging task. Often, we find ourselves trapped in patterns of thought and behavior shaped by the collective beliefs of those around us. To break free from this cycle, we need to venture beyond our comfort zones and embrace new ways of thinking and believing.

Reflect on my own experience with a limiting belief about my voice, inherited from my mother's words. She frequently told me my voice was too loud, too raspy, resembling that of a boy. Growing up with three brothers, my voice seemed to mirror theirs.

"You need to fix your voice," she would insist. Her words became an incessant inner critic in my mind, convincing me that my voice was indeed too loud and rough. This perception persisted until a professional experience – recording a podcast – led to a revelation. Listening to my recorded voice, I was astonished to find it gentle, almost too soft for the impactful messages I wanted to share. This moment highlighted how beliefs, often external, can significantly shape and steer our lives.

The realm of beliefs and the "IT Factor" goes beyond thoughts; it encompasses self-betrayal and self-sabotage. For instance, procrastination often stems from doubts about our worthiness and feelings of being impostors. However, these are beliefs, not immutable truths. By acknowledging their power, we can free ourselves from their grip.

Beliefs can act like an anchor, preventing us from drifting too far. Consider elephants chained as babies to restrict their movement. Even when the chains are removed, they remain captive to the belief that they cannot stray far. Similarly, when our beliefs are anchored to someone else's belief system, rather than our own divinity, they constrain our thoughts and actions.

My revelation occurred while working as a counselor in my early thirties. I realized my life was saturated with limiting beliefs. My children's father seemed to check all the boxes of what I considered essential, leading me to believe he was the right partner. Yet, beneath the surface of our seemingly perfect life, conflicting beliefs eroded my sense of self. Feeling like an imposter while living on the prosperous west side of Saginaw, MI, in contrast to my upbringing on the tougher north side streets, this internal conflict overshadowed my achievements and led me to a crucial turning point.

By age 35, I was exhausted, burdened by conflicting beliefs and internal strife. Despite seeming successful, I felt unfulfilled and anxious, constantly fearing everything could collapse at any moment.

At this crucial point, I made a radical decision. I left my relationship with my children's father, quit my job, and let my house go into foreclosure. I embarked on a bold mission to build a successful business, hoping it would be my salvation. Little did I know, this decision would send ripples through my life.

Embarking on entrepreneurship, I learned about the profound impact of beliefs and the necessity to reshape them. During this time, I co-created a program for my business partner's birthday, "25 Motivating Factors to Shape Your Life." This 25-day plan, intended for our audience, transformed my life emotionally and spiritually. After completing it, I adopted a new perspective and began a month of introspection and self-discovery.

In those thirty days, I analyzed every aspect of my life, scrutinizing my relationships and self-beliefs. When I emerged from this isolation, I faced the foreclosure of my home. Financial constraints made it impossible to buy it back, leading to the tough decision to let it go.

Amidst this chaos, I grew closer to my business partner, who was undergoing his own transformation. Our relationship was a turning point, challenging my beliefs about self-worth and deserving love. After ending that relationship, I focused on envisioning my future, developing a thriving business model under the acronym "STOP IT NOW." I took control of my thoughts and reshaped my internal narrative.

But how did I manage this transformation? It centered around self-talk, the "T" in "STOP IT NOW." Self-talk, the internal dialogue we have with ourselves, is influenced by our inner critic, a composite of all criticisms we've faced from others and ourselves throughout our lives.

Growing up, my inner critic was fueled by harsh comments from my mother, childhood friends, and relatives about my appearance, intelligence, voice, and even my lips. These judgments became etched into my psyche, negatively shaping my self-image. They made me play small, diminishing my self-esteem. I turned into a "yes" person, hiding my true self for fear of scrutiny.

I didn't realize then that I had the power to control my inner narrative. The turning point was when I decided to reprogram my mind and rewrite my internal script. I began creating affirmations for myself, recording daily videos to affirm my worth and potential. I even wrote love letters to myself. Gradually, a transformation unfolded, profoundly impacting my life. I want to share this gift with you through my 30-Day Free Affirmation Challenge. You can join at www. shielalittle.com/affirmations.

By changing my self-perception and confronting my inner critic, I stopped narrating my own sob stories. I broke the cycle of negativity that often came with my monthly periods. Instead, I learned to accept and embrace my body's natural rhythms, allowing myself to fully experience my emotions and update my language. I discovered the power to redefine my story with positive self-talk and affirmations – and you can too.

Every morning, we have the opportunity to set the tone for our day with our self-talk. Even in moments of sadness or anger, our internal dialogue shapes our daily experiences. Did you know that each day, your brain processes about 70,000 thoughts, about 90% of which are repetitive? Approximately 70% of these thoughts are based on limited perceptions and beliefs. Essentially, we often operate on an outdated playlist of limiting beliefs and perceptions about the world and our relationships within it.

Imagine your mental playlist as a compilation of everything you've ever heard about yourself and the world. It's time to upgrade this playlist, akin to updating the operating system on your smartphone. Fill those 70% of repetitive thoughts with affirmations and positive programming. By starting your day with empowering thoughts, you will experience a transformative shift in your life.

Your inner critic may still be present, but remember, you have the power to cultivate your inner cheerleader, your own best friend, through positive self-talk. Take moments to be still, meditate, and observe your thoughts without getting attached to them. As you become aware of the mental chatter, it will begin to subside, similar to how children quiet down when they know they're being watched.

Mastering the IT Factor involves another concept I've developed, called the ART of LIFE. This acronym stands for: Become Aware of your inner critic, Release judgment and shift to a neutral space, and take a different action, like telling yourself something positive. You possess the courage to override negative beliefs and to speak from the fullness of your being. Articulate your desires, update your language with affirmations, and live from your highest self. Your life will undoubtedly transform for the better when you embrace this approach.

In the following pages, we'll explore in greater detail the practical aspects of mastering the IT Factor. We'll cover techniques, exercises, and insights that empower you to take control of your inner dialogue and ultimately transform your life. Prepare for a journey filled with self-discovery, growth, and empowerment.

Addressing Your Inner Critic and Elevating Self Talk

Having journeyed through the intricate landscape of assessing your inner critic and enhancing your self-talk, it's essential to provide you with practical insights and tools to effectively navigate this transformation. The IT Factor, as we've discussed, possesses the potential to reshape your beliefs and, consequently, your life. Below, you'll find some pragmatic strategies and advice to assist you on your path to self-improvement:

1. **Self-awareness is Key:** Self-awareness is the first step towards addressing your inner critic. Begin by simply observing your thoughts. When do you hear that critical voice the loudest? Is it during moments of self-doubt, stress, or when faced with challenges? Understanding when and why your inner critic emerges is essential for taming it.

2. **Challenging and Changing Beliefs**: Recognizing and challenging negative or unhelpful beliefs is a crucial step in overcoming the influence of the inner critic. Cognitive-behavioral techniques, therapy, and self-reflection can help identify and change detrimental beliefs.

3. **Challenge Your Inner Critic:** As you become aware of your inner critic's voice, start challenging its validity. Ask yourself whether the criticisms are based on facts or unfounded beliefs. Are they rooted in your past or projected fears about the future? By critically evaluating these thoughts, you can defuse their power.

4. **Practice Self-Compassion:** Cultivate self-compassion by treating yourself with the same kindness and understanding that you would offer a dear friend. When you make a mistake or fall short of your

expectations, respond with self-compassion rather than harsh self-criticism. This practice can gradually weaken your inner critic's influence.

5. **Reframe Negative Thoughts:** Transform negative self-talk into positive affirmations. When you catch yourself thinking, "I'm not good enough," replace it with, "I am constantly growing and improving." Repetition is key here; the more you affirm your worth, the more you'll believe it.

6. **Journaling:** Keep a journal to record your inner thoughts and emotions. This practice allows you to externalize your inner critic's voice and gain perspective. Analyze the patterns in your journal, noticing recurring themes and triggers. This insight can be invaluable for dismantling your inner critic.

7. **Seek Support:** Don't hesitate to reach out to a trusted friend, family member, or therapist when your inner critic becomes overwhelming. Sometimes, sharing your thoughts and receiving feedback can provide clarity and comfort.

8. **Meditation and Mindfulness:** Incorporate mindfulness and meditation practices into your daily routine. These techniques can help you observe your thoughts without judgment and create mental space between you and your inner critic. Over time, you'll gain better control over your thought patterns.

9. **Positive Self-Affirmations:** Craft a list of positive

affirmations that resonate with you. These should counteract your inner critic's negative messages. Recite these affirmations daily, especially during moments of self-doubt or stress.

10. **Visualization:** Picture your ideal self and the life you desire. Visualization techniques can reinforce positive self-talk and motivate you to take action toward your goals.

11. **Professional Guidance:** If your inner critic is deeply ingrained or severely impacting your life, consider seeking guidance from a mental health professional. They can provide tailored strategies and support to help you overcome self-limiting beliefs.

Remember, addressing your inner critic and improving self-talk is an ongoing journey. Be patient and compassionate with yourself as you work to rewire your thought patterns. Your inner landscape is like a garden; it requires consistent care and nurturing. Over time, you'll witness the blossoming of a more confident, empowered, and self-loving you.

The next chapter will explore further techniques and insights to help you continue your personal development journey. Stay committed to the process, and your IT Factor will shine brighter each day.

"Ideas are essentially your beliefs -- what you believe this world is and what the world does. These beliefs trigger emotions, which trigger behaviors."

SHIELA LITTLE
@IAMSHAPINGSOLUTIONS

"A belief is like this – it anchors you to limitations or abundance, and you function through that lens."

SHIELA LITTLE
@IAMSHAPINGSOLUTIONS

"Self-talk is about your inner conversations; we develop self-love by understanding, accepting, and having compassion for who you are from the inside out."

SHIELA LITTLE
@IAMSHAPINGSOLUTIONS

"We all have the power to redefine our story using affirmations. Start writing down affirmations and love letters. You will soon begin to sense a shift."

SHIELA LITTLE
@IAMSHAPINGSOLUTIONS

6

STOP IT NOW: UNLEASHING YOUR INNER STRENGTH: THE POWER OF NON-NEGOTIABLE

n our exploration of the STOP IT NOW framework, we have journeyed through the "STOP" phase, delving deep into the realms of our past—including our beliefs, thoughts, feelings, and behaviors. We then transitioned to the "IT" phase, focusing on our present internal dialogue about these past experiences. Now, we stand on the brink of the future with the "NOW" phase. This phase is centered on guiding you toward the future you aspire to and rightfully deserve. In the forthcoming three chapters, I will reveal the straightforward yet impactful steps that have transformed both my life and the lives of my clients. These steps are designed to steer us towards the lives we yearn for and are worthy of.

This chapter focuses on a crucial element in personal growth and development—understanding your non-negotiables, symbolized by the 'N' in STOP IT NOW.

Embracing this principle played a pivotal role in guiding me toward an authentic life filled with self-respect while also helping me establish and maintain healthy boundaries. Many people talk about setting boundaries and defending them, but I believe it's essential to distinguish between emotional walls and boundaries.

Emotional walls are often erected as a defense mechanism, shielding us from emotional pain and vulnerability. They manifest as an unwillingness to open up, share our feelings, or maintain emotional closeness due to past hurts, resulting in stories and beliefs that reinforce these walls. However, there are instances when emotional walls can be beneficial— when we need time to process our emotions or when we encounter toxic or harmful individuals. Nevertheless, if these walls become too rigid or towering, they obstruct meaningful connections, often leaving us feeling isolated and alone.

Boundaries, on the other hand, serve as a healthier means to protect our emotional well-being. We set boundaries to safeguard our physical, emotional, and mental health. For example, a boundary might involve graciously declining an invitation when we lack the energy or limiting our time with specific individuals or in certain situations. These boundaries empower us to stay true to ourselves, prioritizing our needs while nurturing healthy relationships with others.

Distinguishing between emotional walls and boundaries can be complex, requiring self-reflection and self-awareness.

While emotional walls may serve us temporarily, recognizing when they hinder our connections is vital. Setting and preserving boundaries can be challenging, but they are indispensable for our well-being and the health of our relationships.

The next time you encounter these terms, remember that emotional walls and boundaries are different. Furthermore, understanding your non-negotiables forms the bedrock for creating healthy boundaries while dismantling emotional walls is the key to cultivating profound and meaningful connections with those around us.

My Path to Non-Negotiables:

Growing up, my home was a place where boundaries were frequently disregarded. Emotional walls were wielded as a form of punishment, and co-dependency was the norm. These dynamics explained many of the behaviors and beliefs I held. I reached a point where I realized that I needed to regain control over my life. It was time to break free from the cycle of co-dependency and victimhood. I yearned to be authentic and embrace my true self, rather than merely playing prescribed roles. This realization marked the beginning of my exploration into non-negotiables.

The environment I grew up in had compelled me to construct emotional walls, more like fortresses than simple lines in the sand. To progress and become my authentic self,

I had to surmount these self-imposed barriers that hindered my engagement with both myself and the world. I needed to move beyond merely saying "stop" and take the necessary steps to break free from detrimental patterns. I no longer wanted to be the victim; I aspired to be me. This quest required me to determine what was right for me rather than adhering to others' notions of right and wrong. Identifying my non-negotiables became paramount.

I realized the need to remain conscious of my emotions in various situations. If someone made me feel a certain way, it was imperative to decipher those feelings and thoughts, understanding how they related to my core belief. I could no longer project my insecurities onto others and assume a passive victim role as if life was merely happening to me. Instead, I needed to embrace the notion that life was happening for me. I learned to acknowledge and release even the minutest discrepancies misaligned with my true self. Operating at 80% because I accepted behaviors, both from myself and others, that did not align with my essence was no longer acceptable. I deserved to operate at 100%, all the time, or as much as possible. And I had to understand what that 100% truly looked like for me.

My goal was to accept myself unconditionally, regardless of others' opinions. I embarked on a journey to strengthen my self-confidence, nurture my self-love, and cultivate the most vital relationship—the one with myself. In essence, I had to cease accepting anything less than what I rightfully deserved from both myself and others.

In my early years, I lacked a clear understanding of what I wouldn't accept in relationships. Conventional dating "rules" often suggested that I needed to conform to a partner's desires for a relationship to succeed. Regrettably, I acquiesced, fearing that asserting my needs would brand me as high-maintenance. This complacency proved unsustainable, as it compromised my self-worth and left me yearning for something more.

One pivotal moment occurred when I embarked on a romantic relationship with a close friend. Initially, we respected each other's personal space, fostering a harmonious dynamic. However, over time, the balance shifted. He began dictating my actions, controlling my choice of friends, and reacting without leaving room for resolution. It was then that I recognized the importance of establishing non-negotiables. I had taken charge of crafting a new life for myself, and it was up to me to determine what I truly desired.

Another turning point came when I made the conscious choice to develop a healthy co-parenting relationship with my children's father. It required me to accept him as he was, letting go of any lingering animosity, regardless of my feelings. Pressuring him to conform to my expectations would only yield temporary results and jeopardize our ability to maintain a long-term, stable environment for our children. This called for a radical shift in perspective.

Following a discussion about our mutual needs, I moved back in with him, focusing on the needs of our children. I clearly defined my non-negotiables, set boundaries, and presented my terms founded on mutual respect and shared needs. At the time, he worked the night shift while I balanced my business pursuits with a Ph.D. program. I proposed that he hire my business to manage his affairs due to his demanding schedule, a suggestion he readily accepted. A year later, our co-parenting relationship had improved significantly, and I was able to handle our conflicts with a lot more ease.

My pledge to myself was clear—I would appreciate his strengths, refrain from judging his shortcomings, and accept him for who he was, not who I wished him to be. Consequently, our partnership gained newfound clarity, fostering a healthy co-parenting environment and unveiling unexpected acts of generosity from my children's father. His initial intention to make a donation to my non-profit eventually culminated in a check double the amount he had initially promised. It was truly a remarkable moment. Understanding what I refused to compromise on in my life illuminated the path to my true desires, allowing us to create mutually beneficial outcomes.

What brought about this transformation? It wasn't an external change but rather a shift in my mindset. We remained the same two individuals, living under the same conditions, yet our relationship underwent a profound transformation. I came to terms with the fact that he would never be the man or husband I might have wished for, given our differences in emotional capacity and understanding of relationships. I refused to continue compromising my life based on his terms, beliefs, or values—none of which were inherently "bad" but misaligned with my own.

The power of non-negotiables also revealed itself in my relationship with my father. He had a habit of emotionally stonewalling me when upset, leading to frequent misunderstandings. For years, our conversations were centered around us conversing on the phone about life situations and circumstances. Although I would visit him periodically, I didn't stay long. Despite our strong bond, he would often resort to passive-aggressive behavior if I didn't meet his expectations or fulfill his requests. His response would leave me feeling guilty for saying no, and I'd eventually succumbed to his demands to avoid tension.

Shortly before the onset of the Covid pandemic, he fell seriously ill and spent a week in the hospital. My sister, Benita, (bless her soul), was known for her nurturing nature and had been the one who would usually care for him. She visited him regularly, often brought him food when she cooked, and maintained constant communication when she lived in the same town as us. However, her relocation left a void. When he fell seriously ill, my sister was no longer there to do the things that she would normally do. Understanding this, I stepped in to visit him during his hospitalization. Upon his return home, I didn't continue my physical visits, I would call to check on him, assuming he had the physical support he needed. On his birthday, I stopped by to see him, and his distant and irritable demeanor caught me by surprise. The tense encounter revealed his dissatisfaction with my actions, and it became evident that he had anticipated me to fill my sister's role as the nurturer. Instead of communicating his feelings to me, he voiced his dissatisfaction with my actions to others. This led to a four-month period of strained communication.

Eventually, I confronted my father, urging him to articulate his expectations clearly. I made it clear that I would not be manipulated or stone-walled and stressed about not being my sister. I communicated my boundaries and explained why it was essential for him to see me for who I truly was rather than projecting his desires onto me. Following this conversation, our relationship took a positive turn; his treatment of me changed significantly, and our relationship improved remarkably.

What instigated this transformation? Again, it wasn't an external change but rather a shift in my mindset. We remained the same two individuals in the same circumstances, yet our relationship underwent a profound transformation. I came to terms with the fact that my father would be set in some ways that I had no power or authority to change. I had to accept our differences and understand the importance of our relationship. I refused to base my behaviors on his ideas of who he wanted me to be and be guilted into behaviors that did not align with my beliefs or values—none of which were inherently "bad" but misaligned with my own.

These examples underscore the profound impact of embracing non-negotiables. By defining and upholding our boundaries, we empower ourselves to live authentically and assertively, free from the constraints of external expectations.

The Power of Non-Negotiables:

I can personally attest to the efficacy of the STOP IT NOW framework. The 'NOW' phase represents the moment when we actively craft our future selves. As the saying goes, you can't pour new wine into old wineskins. You must be willing to become the change you want to see in the world. It will alter the trajectory of your life.

In conclusion, understanding and applying non-negotiables are vital for personal growth and meaningful relationships. They help you assert your worth, protect your well-being, and lead an authentic life. As you embark on your journey, remember: You deserve to operate at 100%, not a fraction less. Your non-negotiables will guide you there.

Insights for Your Journey:

Now that we've explored the concept of non-negotiables and the importance of boundaries, it's time to reflect on how these principles can transform your life. Here are some insights to help you on your journey:

1. **Self-Reflection:** Take time to identify your emotional walls and distinguish them from healthy boundaries. Self-awareness is the first step toward positive change.

2. **Accept Your Feelings**: Understand that your feelings are valid. If something or someone makes you feel a certain way, it's worth exploring why. This self-awareness can guide your decision-making.

3. **Know your values**: Understanding your values is important when setting boundaries because it provides a clear framework for determining what is acceptable and respectful behavior in your relationships and interactions with others. Here's why it matters:

   1. Alignment and Authenticity: Understanding your values ensures that your boundaries reflect what is truly important to you. This leads to more authentic and meaningful interactions with others.

   2. Clarity and Communication: Knowing your values helps you communicate your boundaries more clearly, as you can articulate why certain behaviors or situations are important or unacceptable to you.

   3. Empowerment and Well-being: Setting boundaries

based on your values empowers you to protect your well-being, prioritize what matters most, and maintain self-respect in your relationships.

4. Avoiding Resentment and Frustration: When you set boundaries that align with your values, you're less likely to feel resentful or frustrated because you're upholding what matters most to you. This can lead to healthier and more satisfying relationships.

4. **Embrace Authenticity:** Strive to be your authentic self, free from societal expectations or outdated "rules or beliefs." Authenticity empowers you to set non-negotiables that align with your true values.

5. **Prioritize Self-Worth:** Building your self-worth and confidence is essential. Remember that you deserve to be treated with respect and kindness in all your relationships.

6. **Empower Yourself:** Realize that you have the power to shape your future. By embracing your non-negotiables and setting healthy boundaries, you can create the life you desire and deserve.

As you embark on this journey of self-discovery and personal development, keep these insights in mind. Your non-negotiables are your compass, guiding you towards a life filled with authenticity, self-respect, and meaningful connections.

"Distinguishing between emotional walls and boundaries can be complex, requiring self-reflection and self-awareness."

SHIELA LITTLE
@IAMSHAPINGSOLUTIONS

"I had to cease accepting anything less than what I rightfully deserved from myself and others."

SHIELA LITTLE
@IAMSHAPINGSOLUTIONS

"Understanding what I refused to compromise on in my life illuminated the path to my true desires."

SHIELA LITTLE
@IAMSHAPINGSOLUTIONS

"By defining and upholding our boundaries, we empower ourselves to live authentically and assertively, free from the constraints of external expectations."

SHIELA LITTLE
@IAMSHAPINGSOLUTIONS

7

STOP IT NOW: "AWAKENING POSSIBILITIES: TURN YOUR OBSTACLES INTO OPPORTUNITY"

At this stage of the journey, it's time to wholeheartedly open your mind to the myriad of opportunities that lie before you. This is your moment to craft a blueprint or strategy for moving ahead in life, leaving no room for doubt or hesitation. By transforming your obstacles into opportunities, you're stepping into the realm of change at its deepest level. This step follows the establishment of your non-negotiables because it's essential to shape your mindset and know your values to achieve lasting transformation.

As an entrepreneur, I learned that launching and managing a business was arduous. It demanded unwavering commitment, relentless hard work, and boundless perseverance. Yet, I hadn't fully grasped the profound influence of my mindset on my journey to success.

Your mindset forms the tapestry of thoughts and beliefs

that color your attitudes and shape your behaviors. It's the invisible force that determines how you approach challenges, cope with setbacks, and seize opportunities. When I embarked on my entrepreneurial venture, I realized that my mindset was not aligned with the life I aspired to lead.

Two primary categories often come into play in the realm of mindset: the fixed mindset and the growth mindset. These mindsets encapsulate distinct cognitive approaches to life's challenges, and their influence extends deeply into one's personal and professional evolution.

In simpler terms, it all boils down to how we perceive learning and self-improvement:

Fixed Mindset:

- **Core Beliefs/How They Think:** Some individuals believe that their abilities, intelligence, and talents are fixed and unchangeable.
- **Challenges:** People with a fixed mindset tend to shy away from challenges, driven by a fear of failure. They avoid difficult endeavors, fearing that making mistakes labels them as inadequate.
- **Response to Setbacks and Mistakes:** In the face of adversity or errors, individuals with a fixed mindset may readily give up, viewing their limitations rather than the potential for growth.

- **View on Effort:** Some believe that trying too hard indicates a lack of natural talent, and they may perceive effort negatively.
- **Feedback:** They may not welcome constructive criticism, interpreting it as a verdict of inadequacy.
- **Others' Success:** Rather than finding inspiration in the accomplishments of others, those with a fixed mindset may feel threatened, envious, or convinced they can never achieve similar feats.

Growth Mindset:

- **Core Belief/How They Think:** Those with a growth mindset believe that abilities and intelligence can evolve through dedication, learning, and diligence. They see potential for growth and refinement in all aspects of life.
- **Confronting Challenges:** Those embracing the growth mindset view challenges as opportunities for enrichment. They see challenges as a means to expand their competencies and relish the chance to learn and improve.
- **Dealing with Failures:** Mistakes and failures don't deter them. They consider errors as 'miss-takes,' not condemnations of their abilities. Failures serve as stepping stones for enhancement.

- **View on Effort:** Effort is seen as the pathway to success. Those with a growth mindset are willing to invest the sweat equity required for triumph.
- **Attitude Toward Feedback:** Even if critical, feedback is valued as an invaluable tool for growth and skill development.
- **Reaction to Others' Success:** Instead of feeling threatened by others' accomplishments, those with a growth mindset draw inspiration, believing in their capacity to reach similar heights through dedication and continuous learning.

A growth-oriented mindset is the compass that perceives challenges as opportunities for growth, embraces learning and development, and remains open to new ideas and perspectives. This mindset equips you to take calculated risks, bounce back from failures, and persevere when the going gets tough.

In contrast, a fixed mindset sees challenges as threats, resists risk, and remains closed off to novel ideas and perspectives. Such a mindset can confine your growth and thwart you from unlocking your full potential.

It's crucial to remember that mindsets are not strictly binary; they can exist along a spectrum, with individuals displaying elements of both mindsets in various facets of their lives.

However, understanding these mindsets can enhance

self-awareness, assisting individuals in reshaping thought patterns and nurturing a growth mindset. This mindset is closely linked to heightened resilience, adaptability, and a greater willingness to tackle personal and professional challenges.

So, what can you do to cultivate a growth-oriented mindset so that you can start turning your obstacles into opportunities? Here are a few actionable tips:

- **Embrace a "Growth Mindset" Mentality:** Believe in your capacity to learn and grow from every experience, including failures.
- **Focus on the Positive:** Instead of dwelling on setbacks or negative experiences, seek the silver lining and extract valuable lessons.
- **Stay Curious:** Actively seek new ideas, perspectives, and experiences to broaden your horizons and challenge your beliefs.
- **Be Persistent:** Refuse to give up at the first sign of adversity. Persistence often leads to breakthroughs.

Remember that your mindset can be the decisive factor between success and failure. Cultivating a growth-oriented mindset equips you to navigate challenges effectively and, ultimately, realize your aspirations. To craft your desired mindset and map out your life's blueprint, the TWOS acronym proves invaluable—Triggers, Wins, Obstacles, Strengths/Strategy.

Understanding your triggers, recognizing your wins, identifying your obstacles and embracing your strengths are pivotal steps in shaping the mindset you aspire to embody. Armed with this awareness, you can approach every situation with an open mind, charting a clear course for navigating your personal journey.

Reflecting on my entrepreneurial journey, I vividly recall my early days in 2014 when I operated my business single-handedly. While tasks I enjoyed thrived, those I disliked lingered. This reluctance to tackle certain aspects posed challenges for my business and hampered my progress.

Then came the turning point—a substantial contract at a school to work with students. I cherished this opportunity, but the paperwork that followed proved my Achilles' heel. The hours I invested and the earnings I made unveiled a stark truth—I was essentially making just $12 per hour. Amidst this reflection, I had limited time for family or fun. I feared asking for help, and this belief needed to shift for me to embrace success and pursue my passions. Not being present for my family triggered a feeling of incompetence, and I had to unearth the entrenched beliefs that kept me rooted in this fixed mindset.

Confronting paperwork was another hurdle, as it hadn't been completed efficiently, potentially tarnishing the program's reputation. My belief that I must do everything to feel competent fueled my hesitation to ask for help. Addressing the stress and judgment I faced, I embarked on a journey of self-discovery. My desire to explore ways to manage my responsibilities was critical. By my third year of business, I had decided to delegate tasks and hired someone to assist with paperwork. This seemingly minor adjustment became transformative. It helped me overcome obstacles and paved the way for new opportunities.

Identifying my areas of strength rekindled my sense of purpose and honed my ability to invest my time, energy, and emotions purposefully. Henceforth, I delegated tasks outside my sphere of enjoyment, and my performance flourished. Though a fraction of my earnings went to others, I had gained something invaluable—clarity.

Similarly, I encountered another win by reassessing my perspective on domestic duties. Cleaning, in particular, was a task I disliked but felt obligated to perform, thanks to deep-seated beliefs about femininity. Recognizing my resources and the ability to hire someone to maintain my home sparked a transformative shift. I liberated myself from chores that triggered emotional turmoil, enabling me to reclaim time for activities I cherished.

Reflecting on my past, I realized that the seeds of this knowledge had always existed within me, even if not fully acknowledged. At the tender age of 14, I became the family breadwinner through my hairstyling skills. My familial obligations, however, demanded I perform household chores as well. Instead of personally fulfilling these tasks, I paid my brothers to do them—a solution that had unintended consequences. My mother's words echoed in my ears—her prediction that I'd never find a husband due to my lack of desire to perform culinary or homemaking skills. Over time, these words triggered discomfort in my interactions and relationships with men. I grappled with a fixed mindset shaped by my mother, grandmother, and other female figures in my family. Despite acknowledging my non-domesticated nature, I was compelled to act otherwise.

The turning point arrived when I confronted this obstacle head-on. Armed with my TWOS assessment, I discerned what was triggering me: the overwhelming responsibility of being a mother, a homemaker, and a businesswoman. Reflecting on my wins (desires), I understood the satisfaction that accompanied a clean house. Identifying obstacles, such as limited time and hesitations about seeking assistance, led me to pinpoint my strengths—my financial means, which allowed me to create a strategy—delegate.

It wasn't a matter of lacking domestic skills; it was about the emotional triggers and inefficient use of my time associated with these tasks. Hiring someone to handle cleaning became a win, granting me more time for enjoyable pursuits. Once a chore, cooking evolved into a therapeutic and enjoyable activity, fostering healthier relationships when shared with a partner.

A similar shift occurred when I embarked on the quest to define my purpose and determine the balance between therapy and coaching. The answer was clear—coaching. Guiding individuals towards success by helping them overcome obstacles and discover their wins became my passion.

Armed with the insights revealed by the TWOS framework, I felt empowered to make decisions that aligned with my values. This newfound clarity heightened my happiness and productivity and enhanced my role as a mother. I realized that my understanding of what it meant to be a parent and my role in my sons' lives needed redefining.

I recognized a pattern that was evident when I became the family breadwinner at 14. Chores may not have been my forte, but I have always possessed the drive to excel in my chosen field. The same principle held true as I navigated the complexities of my professional life. A willingness to delegate tasks outside my sphere of enjoyment allowed me to flourish and gain the gift of clarity and purpose.

My journey didn't end there. Learning to turn my obstacles into opportunities allowed me to confront deeply ingrained beliefs about femininity and domestic duties, realizing that my role as a woman extended beyond traditional expectations. With newfound freedom from these constraints, I invested quality time in my children, fostered deep connections in my relationships, and relished the simple joys of life.

Once you've identified your values and desires, it's crucial to assess whether your mindset aligns with your aspirations. You'll begin to unearth the principles that form the foundation for manifesting the life you yearn for. Many people find themselves adrift in the sea of life, out of sync with this perspective.

My transformed mindset allowed me to embrace guiding principles that everything is working for my ultimate good. The concept of the law of attraction, mirrored in various spiritual teachings, became evident. What you emit into the universe returns to you because where your attention goes, energy flows.

Your life remains stagnant if you focus on negativity, ruminate on fixed beliefs, or doubt change. My simple yet potent principles and growth mindset fortified my resolve to remain unbroken during dark times. While storms may rage, I found solace in the belief that they ultimately serve my greater good.

I want to emphasize that I never gave up, and neither should you. Your purpose and desire will stand you up when passion breaks you down. My steadfast commitment to my purpose and desires fuels my journey. I stand firmly in my purpose and understand my desires, and I encourage you to embark on the same self-discovery.

Autonomy, divinity, integrity, trust, fidelity, love, creativity, my family, and communication are values that I hold in high esteem. While treating others as I would like to be treated is the bedrock of my guiding principles. Take a moment to discover what you value and the guiding principles that resonate with you, and watch as your life transforms in profound ways.

Opening your mind is an exploration of the TWOS framework—a potent framework to help you turn your obstacles into opportunities. To reinforce these newfound perspectives, create affirmations that reprogram your subconscious, reinforcing your self-belief. Remember, belief is the cornerstone of everything. Have faith, put in the work, and understand that you are intrinsically worthy of all you desire.

The power of an open mind is boundless. It propels us to explore the uncharted territories of our potential and embrace the richness of life's offerings. As you embark on this transformative journey, remember the keys to unlocking your fullest potential—embracing a growth mindset, reflecting on your TWOS, and defining your values and guiding principles.

With an open mind, there are no limits to what you can achieve. Embrace the change, trust the process, and know that your desires are within reach. Your newfound mindset, values, guiding principles, and unwavering belief in yourself illuminate your path.

Cultivating an Open Mindset for Opportunities, Healing, and Growth

An open mindset is the key to recognizing opportunities, healing, and personal growth. It allows you to embrace change, learn from your experiences, and unlock your full potential. Here are some essential steps to help you develop and nurture an open mindset:

1. **Self-awareness**: Start by becoming aware of your current mindset. Are you more inclined toward a fixed mindset or a growth mindset? Recognize your thought patterns, beliefs, and reactions to challenges.

2. **Challenge Your Beliefs**: Question your existing beliefs about yourself and your abilities. Are there limiting beliefs that are holding you back? Identify them and challenge their validity. Remember that beliefs are not facts; they can be changed.

3. **Embrace Challenges:** Instead of avoiding challenges, welcome them as opportunities for growth. Understand that setbacks and failures are part of the journey toward healing and personal development. Each challenge you face is a chance to learn and improve.

4. **Learn from Mistakes:** Shift your perspective on mistakes. See them as "mis-takes" that provide valuable lessons rather than failures. When you make a mis-take, ask yourself, "What can I learn from this?"

Use your setbacks as stepping stones toward your goals.

5. **Stay Curious:** Cultivate curiosity about the world and your own potential. Explore new ideas, perspectives, and experiences. A curious mind is open and always eager to learn and grow.

6. **Positive Self-Talk:** Be mindful of your inner dialogue. Replace self-criticism with self-compassion. Treat yourself with the same kindness and encouragement you would offer a friend.

7. **Seek Feedback:** Welcome feedback from others and see it as an opportunity for growth. Constructive criticism can provide valuable insights and help you improve. Don't view feedback as a personal attack.

8. **Set Realistic Goals:** Establish achievable goals that align with your values and desires. Break them down into smaller, manageable steps. Celebrate your progress along the way.

9. **Practice Resilience:** Develop emotional resilience to bounce back from setbacks. Cultivate a mindset that sees obstacles as opportunities rather than insurmountable barriers.

10. **Mindfulness and Meditation:** Engage in mindfulness practices and meditation to quiet the mind and create mental space for openness. These practices can help you stay present, reduce anxiety, and foster a receptive mindset.

11. **Surround Yourself with Positive People:** Spend time with people who support your growth and have open mindsets themselves. Positive relationships can reinforce your commitment to personal development.

12. **Gratitude: Practice gratitude daily.** Focus on the things you're thankful for in your life. Gratitude can shift your perspective and help you appreciate the opportunities that an open mindset brings.

Remember that developing an open mindset is an ongoing journey. It takes time and practice, but the rewards are transformative. As you open your mind to new possibilities, you'll discover that healing and personal growth become attainable and immensely fulfilling. Your life can be a canvas where you paint the masterpiece of your dreams, one open-minded stroke at a time.

"Your mindset is the compass that guides your journey; it's up to you whether it points to uncharted possibilities or familiar limitations."

SHIELA LITTLE
@IAMSHAPINGSOLUTIONS

"In the realm of growth, challenges are the stepping stones to transformation, and setbacks are simply setups for comebacks."

SHIELA LITTLE
@IAMSHAPINGSOLUTIONS

"Success isn't determined by the absence of obstacles but by your willingness to turn them into opportunities."

SHIELA LITTLE
@IAMSHAPINGSOLUTIONS

"Your mindset shapes your world, and with the right mindset, even storms can be seen as opportunities for growth and renewal."

SHIELA LITTLE
@IAMSHAPINGSOLUTIONS

"To open your mind is to open the door to a world of limitless possibilities; the only limits are the ones you set for yourself."

SHIELA LITTLE
@IAMSHAPINGSOLUTIONS

8

STOP IT NOW: "MANIFESTING YOUR FUTURE WITH A WIN/WHEN ATTITUDE"

In my personal life and business endeavors, I've always held a fundamental principle close to my heart: "Start at the beginning with the end in mind." Why? Because this simple phrase encapsulates the intention and purpose behind everything we do. It provides us with an unwavering anchor for our visions, a beacon to guide us forward even in the face of inevitable challenges. And as we delve into the final chapter of our journey through the STOP IT NOW framework, remember that this chapter is just as pivotal as the first.

I vividly recall a moment during my life's journey when my higher self, intricately connected to the Source of all things, posed a profound question: "What does having the faith of a mustard seed mean to you?" This question came to me on a day when I felt overwhelmed, seeking direction on how to more effectively navigate toward my goals.

In my mind, I initially thought, "It means having a little faith, just enough to get by." But then, a deeper truth emerged: "Having faith like a mustard seed means believing that the seed will grow into the fullness of a mustard tree." At that instant, I experienced a profound shift. I realized that faith wasn't just about holding onto a small belief; it was about envisioning my full potential and unwaveringly believing that I could and would become that person. The critical question then became, what does my fullness entail, and how can I comprehend its form and substance?

The 'W' in 'STOP IT NOW' represents 'Win-When.' It's about defining what a WIN looks like in all areas of our lives and identifying the exact moments we aim to achieve these victories. It also involves recognizing the habits, beliefs, and behaviors that need nurturing, transformation, or release. A wise coach once said that people often overestimate what they can achieve in a year and underestimate what they can accomplish in three. Therefore, I committed to becoming the person I needed to be to win, giving myself ample time for this transformation—a period for cultivating my aspirations, learning, and growing.

This chapter is a gateway to expanding your mind. Many of us are stuck in a state of inertia, shaped by our habits, which in turn, define our identities. To break free, we must start by asking the right questions. What are your personal 'WIN' questions? These are more than just words; they are the keys to self-discovery. What do you truly want for yourself, free from external influences? What is your vision for your best self? These questions should resonate across all aspects of your life—health, finances, relationships, friendships, career, and more. This holistic approach allows you to address your entire being, not just parts of it.

I understand the inner conflict when our goals seem at odds with our capabilities. I once longed for financial security but felt it was unattainable, conflicting with my desire to be a present mother, partner, and friend. This tension led to guilt and the belief that I had to choose one over the other. It wasn't just about financial stability; my perceptions of men as unfaithful and self-absorbed created a gap between what I desired in a partner and the stereotypes I believed in.

A similar struggle manifested in my relationship with money. I longed for a stress-free, wealthy life, yet my understanding of money was associated with relentless toil and the belief that 'easy come, easy go.' The turning point came when I dedicated time to define my aspirations in all areas of life, while critically examining my beliefs about myself and each category. This process helped me align with my true desires and prepared me to manifest the abundance I sought and deserved.

When you reach a decision's precipice and gain clarity on your highest aspirations, transformation begins. As the saying goes, 'a rising tide lifts all boats.' In your zone, creating an impact feels effortless and natural. This doesn't mean you'll be free from emotional challenges associated with leaving behind your old life, self, and relationships. It means that navigating life's storms becomes more manageable. Procrastination often serves as a refuge from the emotions tied to daunting tasks or changes. The real challenge is mastering these emotions, stepping into the light, and aligning with your authentic self. That's where magic unfolds, and life becomes less burdensome. For instance, during a high-performance coaching program, I achieved my goals but felt an unsettling dissonance. Despite having everything I envisioned, my life wasn't aligned with my desired way of living. My dreams were grand—I wanted financial freedom, a 25K+ monthly income, property ownership, and to launch a class on emotional intelligence (which became the STOP IT NOW program). The question was, how could I bridge the gap?

My coach challenged me with questions: What must I stop doing to achieve these goals? How should I show up? What steps must I take? The answers were not as straightforward as I thought. While discipline, faith, and letting go seemed logical, the underlying issue was that I operated from a scarcity mindset.

A scarcity mindset is when someone constantly thinks there's not enough of something—whether it's money, time, love, or success. They often feel worried and believe that resources are limited, so they might hoard things and find it hard to share or take risks. This mindset makes them focus on what they don't have rather than appreciating what they do have. It can create stress and stop them from seeing opportunities or working well with others. Shifting to an abundance mindset means believing there's plenty to go around and seeing opportunities everywhere. It involves appreciating what you have, being open to new things, and thinking positively about what's possible rather than dwelling on limitations.

I needed to STOP my current activities and mindset entirely and become the catalyst for the change I wanted to see. This marked the beginning of my journey into my divine space, harnessing the power of my feminine energy and intelligence. This journey unfolded in alignment with the STOP IT NOW framework. I realized that by embracing God's promises and grace, showing compassion to myself, and focusing on abundance and favor, I could indefinitely unlock my potential.

If you've ever felt broken and resourceless, with a nagging sense that something is 'off,' then this book is your guiding light. Within these pages lies a framework to elevate your awareness and free you from patterns and behaviors holding you back. It's time to rewrite your story, craft your vision, and direct your energy towards the life you desire. Your energy and 750 trillion cells can act as a magnetic force. Your thoughts project into the world, and your heart, the magnet, draws your vision back into your energy field, materializing your dreams. Your heart space, the body's most powerful energy field, radiates energy up to 10 feet away and is a source of your intuition. Begin by unlocking and healing your heart space, a process catalyzed by STOP IT NOW.

Each step in the framework challenges your existing beliefs, dismantles obstacles, and crafts a pathway to ascend to a higher realm of belief and knowing. You are prepared for this moment. Embrace the clarity you've gained through these potent steps and brace yourself for profound change. While this chapter marks the end of the book, it heralds the beginning of your journey towards living the life you truly want and undoubtedly deserve.

Cultivating a Winning Mindset

As we conclude this chapter, it's crucial to delve into the art of cultivating a winning mindset. Developing a winning mindset isn't just about setting goals; it's a profound shift in the way you perceive yourself and your potential. Let's explore some key insights to help you embark on this transformative journey.

1. **Define Your Wins:** It all begins with a clear understanding of what constitutes a win in your life. These wins should be deeply personal and aligned with your values, aspirations, and desires. Take time to reflect on what you genuinely want for yourself, your family, your career, and your overall well-being. Remember, these wins are unique to you, so don't be

swayed by external expectations.

2. **Set Specific Timeframes:** A coach once informed me that we overestimate what we can attain in one year, and we tend to underestimate what can be accomplished in three years. While dreaming big is essential, it's equally crucial to ground your aspirations in reality. The "When" in "Win-When" emphasizes the importance of setting specific timeframes for your goals. This provides a sense of urgency and a roadmap for your journey. Identify when you want to achieve these wins, whether it's one year, three years, or more. Break down your larger goals into smaller, manageable steps with deadlines.

3. **Embrace Grace and Patience:** Achieving your desired wins may not always go according to plan. Life is filled with unexpected twists and turns. During challenging times, it's vital to practice self-compassion. Understand that setbacks and delays are part of the journey. Be patient with yourself and the process. Instead of harsh self-criticism, replace it with self-encouragement and the belief that you can overcome any obstacle.

4. **Cultivate Resilience:** Building a winning mindset also involves developing resilience. Life's challenges can be formidable, but your resilience can be even stronger. Learn from setbacks, bounce back from failures, and use adversity as a stepping stone for

growth. Remember, every obstacle is an opportunity to refine your strategy and move closer to your wins.

5. **Surround Yourself with Support:** You don't have to embark on this journey alone. Seek mentors, coaches, or a supportive community sharing your vision and values. Surrounding yourself with like-minded individuals can provide motivation, guidance, and a sense of belonging.

6. **Maintain a Growth Mindset:** As we discussed in previous chapters, adopting a growth mindset is transformative. Embrace challenges as opportunities for growth, view effort as a path to success, and welcome feedback as a tool for improvement. A growth-oriented mindset can propel you towards your wins with resilience and determination.

7. **Shift to an Abundance Mindset:** Shifting to an abundance mindset involves making conscious changes in your thinking patterns and beliefs. Here are some steps you can take to cultivate an abundance mindset:

   • Practice Gratitude: Start each day by acknowledging and appreciating the things you have in your life. Keep a gratitude journal and write down things you're grateful for regularly. Focusing on what you have can shift your mindset away from scarcity.

   • Challenge Scarcity Thoughts: When you catch

yourself thinking in terms of scarcity (e.g., "There's not enough for everyone"), consciously challenge those thoughts. Instead, reframe them positively (e.g., "There are plenty of opportunities available for me").

- Visualize Success and Abundance: Spend time visualizing your goals and dreams as if they've already been achieved. Envision abundance in your life, whether it's in relationships, career, or personal growth. This visualization can help rewire your brain to focus on possibilities rather than limitations.

- Practice Abundance in Giving: Generosity and giving can reinforce an abundance mindset. Share your time, skills, and resources with others. Contributing to others' well-being can reinforce the belief that there's enough for everyone.

- Avoid Comparisons: Refrain from comparing yourself to others. Everyone's journey is different, and comparing often leads to a scarcity mindset. Focus on your progress and growth rather than someone else's achievements.

- Embrace Challenges and Learn from Failure: See challenges as opportunities for growth rather than setbacks. Embrace failure as a chance to learn and improve. This mindset shift helps you see setbacks as temporary and part of the learning process.

- Surround Yourself with Positivity: Surround yourself with people who have an abundance mindset. Their positivity and outlook can influence your thinking and reinforce a mindset of abundance.
- Practice Mindfulness and Self-Compassion: Mindfulness helps you stay present and appreciate the current moment, while self-compassion allows you to forgive yourself for mistakes and failures, fostering a healthier mindset.

8. **Regularly Reflect and Adjust:** Periodically revisit your wins and the timelines you've set. Life is dynamic, and your goals may evolve. Reflect on your progress, celebrate your achievements, and adjust your strategy as needed. Stay flexible and open to refining your path towards your wins.

In conclusion, developing a winning mindset is an ongoing process that blends ambition with self-compassion, determination with patience, and adaptability with resilience. As you pursue your wins and their associated timelines, remember that the journey itself is a significant part of the transformation. Embrace it fully, and you'll reach your desired wins and discover a newfound sense of purpose and fulfillment along the way. This may mark the end of this chapter, but it's just the beginning of your journey toward living the life you want and truly deserve.

"Start at the beginning with the end in mind. It sets the intention and purpose for everything we do, anchoring our vision even when things get difficult."

SHIELA LITTLE
@IAMSHAPINGSOLUTIONS

"Having faith like a mustard seed means that the seed believes it will become the fullness of the mustard tree."

SHIELA LITTLE
@IAMSHAPINGSOLUTIONS

"When we create habits, then those habits create us. Staying in the same habit or story keeps us stuck. It is about self-discovery – what you want for your highest best self."

SHIELA LITTLE
@IAMSHAPINGSOLUTIONS

"Shifts begin to happen when you become aware of what you want."

SHIELA LITTLE
@IAMSHAPINGSOLUTIONS

"Life becomes easier when you learn how to manage your emotions."

SHIELA LITTLE
@IAMSHAPINGSOLUTIONS

AFTERWORD

Embracing Life's Journey and Shaping Your Success

Reflecting on the incredible journey we've taken together through these pages, I'm reminded that life is a tapestry woven with both triumphs and tribulations. If someone had asked me in my early 20's if I would be where I am today or have the mindset I possess, I might have replied, "I cannot see my life past the age of 27." The odds seemed stacked against me from an early age, but every challenge, obstacle, and hardship I faced has played an integral role in shaping the person I am today.

I firmly believe that God doesn't make mistakes. Miracles surround us daily, a testament to the limitless possibilities that lie before us. God's desire is for us to experience the very best life has to offer, and it's a journey filled with opportunities, both big and small.

If you find yourself hesitant to take bold steps, remember that progress can begin with smaller ones. Fueled by faith, even baby steps can lead you to your destination. As you move forward, life moves with you. Emotions, those powerful currents within us, are simply energy in motion. Your life is like an insatiable appetite, craving nourishment every day, every moment. In times of dis-ease, learn to feed your life with love, attention, and compassion. There is no true end; only an everlasting new beginning is waiting for you.

As you continue to embark on this journey, know that accountability partners can make a world of difference in your healing and self-discovery process. The desire to dream big, retrain your mind, and summon the courage to step into your SPACE (your Spiritual Pattern that is Authentically Creating Energy) is within you. You already possess everything you need; you just have to unlock your potential.

Shaping Solutions (www.shapingsolutions.org) stands ready to be your accountability partner and SUCCESS Coach. We're here to walk alongside you as you embrace your highest and best self, living the life you truly desire and deserve. My story serves not only to share my personal journey but also to inspire and guide you on yours.

Recognizing that not everyone may be ready to dive headfirst into coaching, I've created something special for you: an exclusive workbook that complements my memoir. This resource has been thoughtfully crafted to help you explore your own experiences more deeply, offering actionable steps toward personal growth.

Visit www.stopitnow.online today to access your workbook. It acts as a bridge between the insights from my memoir and the transformational coaching we offer, allowing you to progress at your own pace. Each chapter of our lives contains valuable lessons; this workbook can help you uncover and apply them.

Remember, life is a journey, and every step you take brings you closer to the magnificent, fulfilling life that awaits you. Embrace it, cherish it, and make it your own.

www.ingramcontent.com/pod-product-compliance
Lightning Source LLC
Chambersburg PA
CBHW060528130626
46553CB00002B/681